William Harris Rule

The Holy Sabbath

Instituted in Paradise, and Perfected through Christ (An historical Demonstration)

William Harris Rule

The Holy Sabbath
Instituted in Paradise, and Perfected through Christ (An historical Demonstration)

ISBN/EAN: 9783744757041

Printed in Europe, USA, Canada, Australia, Japan

Cover: Foto ©Lupo / pixelio.de

More available books at **www.hansebooks.com**

THE HOLY SABBATH

INSTITUTED IN PARADISE, AND PERFECTED THROUGH CHRIST.

An Historical Demonstration.

BY
WILLIAM HARRIS RULE, D.D.

"This is the Love of God, that we keep His Commandments: and His Commandments are not grievous."

LONDON:
S. W. PARTRIDGE & CO., 9, PATERNOSTER ROW.

CONTENTS.

		PAGE
	A Word to the Reader ...	5
I.	The Primeval Sabbath ...	9
II.	The Sabbath before the Flood ...	19
III.	From the Deluge to the Exode	23
IV.	The Sabbath Law not Levitical	27
V.	From the Passage of the Jordan to the Babylonish Captivity ...	45
VI.	After the Captivity	54
VII.	The Jewish Sabbath, or Sabbath spoiled with Traditional Observances	61
VIII.	The Jewish Sabbath during our Lord's Ministry ...	74
IX.	Our Lord's Ministrations on the Sabbath-day	86
X.	The Lord's Day, or Christian Sabbath	96
XI.	The Christian Sabbath in the First Three Centuries	112
XII.	Early Diversities of Teaching and Custom	120
XIII.	Romish Perversion of the Fourth Commandment	126
XIV.	Old English Law ...	134
XV.	After the Reformation, on the Continent and in England	140
XVI.	On the Right Observance of God's Law	150

THE HOLY SABBATH.

A WORD TO THE READER.

Courteous Reader,—I will not provoke you to debate. I shall not write a polemical dissertation, nor imagine myself to be engaged in a controversy. I will endeavour to trace faithfully the lines of history, and ascertain the exact force of Divine law. Customs may become obsolete, but facts cannot. I will, therefore, ask you to accept the record of facts, so far as the record is trustworthy, and will, therefore, avoid reference to any source which is not certainly authentic. We bow to the supreme authority of God's law, and ignore, in matters of sacred obligation, the claims of human law and the force of human custom, when custom lacks the sanction of that law which it is our common duty to obey.

One thing I shall not do. I shall not quote modern books, nor trouble myself nor you with detailing the opinions of recent writers. With all due respect for many who have written on the subject, I shall make no allusion to any, beyond the general allusion to one well-known class of writers which will be implied all through. None of our opinions, as opinions only, have the least intrinsic value, nor is it easy to see where place can be fairly found for the intrusion of opinions when we are treating on matters of law and facts of history. Besides, the purchaser of a book on the Sabbath should have a practical end in view, which can only be satisfied by reference to the primary authority. If that object be not attained, so far at least as the honest endeavour of the writer may help to its attainment, the reader will have wasted his money and misemployed his time. I therefore abstain from useless quotations, and endeavour to pass over everything which I consider to be uncertain.

We should agree, I think, not to insist on anything which is doubtful. Things imperfectly known, or not well understood, cannot but be mentioned by the way as incidental or perhaps accessory, yet only mentioned as such, to be estimated at last according to their ascertained value. If not morally sound or historically true, they must sooner or later be rejected. Let us search, then, for historic truth. Let us be on our guard against error in judgment and in practice. There are bigots in the world, we know; there are also cynics and infidels. I would shun both classes; and having now endeavoured to set myself right with you, I pray for clearness of perception, with integrity of principle, and go to work.

THE HOLY SABBATH.

CHAPTER I.

THE PRIMEVAL SABBATH.

The world was created "in the beginning." It floated in space a dark, terrestrial ball indeed. It was *desolate and void*, תֹהוּ וָבֹהוּ. In that imperfect state it could not be the habitation of man, nor of creatures constituted like its present inhabitants. How long that state of desolation and emptiness continued it is impossible to calculate, and it would be idle to conjecture.

Geologists have certainly traced successive changes, but it is not my business to meddle with speculations which have no relation to the present subject, except so far as they justify a limitation of the works described in the Mosaic account of the Creation to six natural days. Earth there was. Air there was, and water. Heat there must have been. There was no radiant light—that is to say, no light proceeding from the luminaries that now shine in the heavens. Darkness was on the face of the deep. If land and sea had ever been distinct, and if there were ever atmospheric phenomena like those with which we are now familiar, that must have all ceased by some act of the Creator before the light we now enjoy was kindled into day, and the world framed and furnished in the order which it now presents.

The Creation described in the Mosaic history occupied six days, during which time the Almighty established the perfect order which has ever since continued. "Thus the heavens "and the earth were finished, and all the host of them. And "on the seventh day God ended his work which He had made; "and He rested on the seventh day from all his work which "He had made. And God blessed the seventh day, and sanc- "tified it: because that in it He had rested from all his work "which God created and made." (Gen. ii. 1—3.) Thus speaks the only history of its birth which the world possesses. The authenticity of this history has often been sharply contested, but as often proved. It harmonizes with subsequent histories, with traditions, and with nature. The institution of the Sabbath was the very first event after the Creation, and we shall immediately enter on the track of evidence which connects that first event with the whole course of time.

On the quotation now made from the second chapter of Genesis it must be noted that the Creator of the ends of the earth, who fainteth not, neither is weary, did not take rest from labour, although He ceased from all his work which He had made. For the word וַיִּשְׁבֹּת does not signify the taking of rest only, nor even chiefly, but the *ceasing from action*. It does not imply sinking into a condition of quiescence. Therefore the idea of Sabbatic rest is not that of the inert exhaustion of a weary workman. It denotes no more than the ceasing from a previous occupation, which is perfectly consistent with entire freedom from fatigue, and unfettered activity in exertion of the mightiest power.

It is said that God *blessed* the seventh day, and *hallowed* it. Now this declaration of what God did is, in effect, a record of one of his most admirable works. Each of the preceding six days was distinguished by a special display of creative power and wisdom. The work of each day is said by the inspired historian to have been pronounced very good: "God saw that it was good." To the eye of the Creator all his works were good. Man, dim-sighted and ill-content, amidst much repining, has often set himself to search out these works, and often, through ages of heathen ignorance, he has mistaken the creatures for the Creator, and deified the workmanship of the Unknown God. In the most enlightened age the wisest men examine these works minutely as they were never before examined, and reverently pronounce them beautiful and perfect beyond the best that they could ever have conceived. From the production of these exquisitely perfect works God ceased, but from his government of the glorious universe He did not for a moment cease.

On the first day of man's existence, counted seventh of that wondrous week which, without it, would not have been complete, our Heavenly Father having created woman also, and revealed his pleasure that in that creation of male and female should be laid the foundation of human society, bestowed his effectual care on its complete establishment. The establishment of society—of which only man is capable—was not effected by any supplementary creation, but by the bestowment of a solemn blessing on the creatures whom He had made in his own image.

God blessed the seventh day. We cannot peruse with intelligence that which is related concerning the six days' works without some apprehension of their majesty, but that is much heightened when we peruse the further account of that first day of the completed world. Surely the preceding sentences of the first Book of Moses cannot be so full of meaning, and this one sentence, "God blessed the seventh "day," be meaningless. We read of other blessings, every one of them great. The blessing of Abraham, for example; valid when given, and valid at the present moment. The blessing is visible in the perpetuation of his family, and the extension of an incalculably precious blessing from a son of Abraham to all the families of the earth. "God said, Let "there be light, and there was light"—the searching light of day; the glorious firmament; the majesty of mountain and of ocean with far extended shores; the all-pervading life of nature animating the specks that play upon the field of the miscroscope; the creatures that people the depths and swarm in the heights above us; the flocks and herds, with every tribe of subject nature. Here is man himself, with his high faculties and varied powers. All these are witnesses to the omnipotence of each of the six days' words; and could the seventh word of benediction be powerless? That could not be. His "rest," as we call it, was not a prostration of power. Creation He had finished, but now He blesses it, and He sanctifies besides. He crowns all his creatures with a blessing, and God's blessing could not be unavailing. What man of us would have his own poor blessing counted for nothing? Or who, if he thought the blessing of a father worth mentioning, would not expect the father's children to cherish the remembrance? Isaac blessed his children, and foretold what the effects would be. Jacob blessed his sons, heads of the future tribes, and predicted the future fruits and proofs of blessing. The Most High God blessed his first-created children, and for their sakes blessed every returning seventh day. And was that blessing barren? Did it leave no mark? If so, then why was it not left unrecorded that it might be forgotten? For if it had conferred no benefit, it would have brought back no praise to Him who gave it.

The thought of an idle blessing from the lips of God is in itself profane, and cannot be entertained without offence. It was not needful for the Father of mankind to couch the benediction in prophetic words, for that would have been to anticipate all prophecies, and recite the yet unspoken tale of his manifold bounty and unfathomable love. But we have learnt enough when we are told that in the hours of the first Sabbath-day in their existence God visited his happy children in Paradise.

How often He repeated the Sabbath visits we have no clue even to conjecture; but we do know that at some time He taught them wherein should lie the sanctity and well-being of their children's homes. He instructed them, for themselves and us, in the duty of mutual fidelity, and gave them a law of innocence. He imparted to his son, our first father, a spirit of wisdom so perfect, and so exact perception, that he could give a name to every living thing according to its kind and uses. We further know that when our first parents abused his gifts, and violated his most plain and gracious law, He did not at once cast them off with a sudden stroke of wrath, but taught them again a new lesson adapted to their altered state.

For all this instruction there should be some time allowed, and what time better than the day of rest, when with undistracted mind they could receive their teachings and have their understanding disciplined into clear perception of all necessary truth? When they were yet without sins, placed at the head of all inferior creatures, and appointed to discharge the duties of their high station, only a little lower than the angels —the blessing of a primeval Sabbath must have been worthy of Him who gave it, and equal to the dignity of them to whom it was given. We may therefore venture to believe that on that first blessed day in the Garden of Eden, with the glory of God in the midst of it, Eden was like Heaven. Although, therefore, the words we read are few, the import of those words is greater than we are able to conceive; and it is beyond all doubt that the revelation of truth from God to man then had its beginning.

The memory of what Adam learned before his fall could not perish. It must have served for his guidance, to be treasured as a family tradition, and to dwell on the lips of his descendants through many generations. In his own breast there was a recollection of the grandeur, the bliss, the holiness of the first Sabbath-day, which the Creator deigned to hallow with his presence in a degree beyond the power of language to express. While the blessing was actual, the hallowing was declared to be prospective also. To *hallow*, קדש, is to set apart. God set apart the seventh day. He did not intend to set it apart at some future time; He did so then. The Sabbath then became a positive institution. His will, then made known, was law. The law was not repealed, nor did it ever fall into desuetude, so far as we know; and if there were any records of the earliest ages extant, we might expect to find therein some trace of its observance or its breach. The probability, however, could only be in proportion to the extent and character of the records, and the intention with which they were made. It is therefore our business to examine such fragments as we have, first noting that, in addition to all that was included in the blessing of that first Sabbath in Paradise, there was a declaration that for the future every seventh day should be set apart, and that all kinds of ordinary work should then be put away. The blessing, it may be fairly inferred, was associated with duty, and we must be careful to observe that in Paradise the duty was established; or, in other words, that Sabbath-keeping was a law of Paradise.

Therefore it is manifest that they are mistaken who say that the commandment to abstain from the forbidden fruit was the only law of Paradise, that the religion of our first parents was but negative, and that to eat or not to eat the apple made up the entire sum of the primeval code of law.

Apart from speculation on the nature and intention of that prohibitory statute, we must carefully consider this part of Divine Revelation, and acknowledge the fact of Divine teaching amidst the solemnities and blessings of a Sabbath in Paradise, whenever we date back to the first seventh day of time. Enough has now been said to remind thoughtful readers of what has never yet been quite forgotten—that that day marks exactly the beginning of the world's Sabbath-keeping, and proves that the law was not delivered to any one portion of the human race more than to another, but to the progenitors of all mankind, on all of whom it is therefore equally binding.

The division of time into weeks, or rather the parcelling of days into weeks, irrespective of the natural divisions of time into lunar months and solar years, has often been marked in relation to the present subject. This hebdomadal division, it is alleged, has prevailed widely among nations that had no knowledge of revealed religion, and it is argued that there must have been a reason for this antecedent to the Hebrew Scriptures—an origin older than the writing of history, even older than Moses, the oldest known writer of the fragments of primeval history preserved in the Book of Genesis, and there only. This would be powerful evidence of the antiquity and universality of the Sabbatic institution, if it could be fairly made out; but, on examining the passages quoted from Greek classics, I do not find them, when read together with their context, at all relevant to this matter. Hesiod or Homer, speaking of the seventh day of the month, cannot be truthfully quoted as referring to that seventh day which is repeated four or five times in every month. Whether the week of the Greeks and Romans, borrowed from the Egyptians, was to be attributed to the primeval Sabbath, or to the worship of the heavenly bodies, of which the chief were the sun, the moon, and the five planets, Mars, Mercury, Jupiter, Venus, and Saturn, is an undecided question; and I am, on my own principle, excluded from any advantage which the preponderance of probability might give me.

The sacred text, understood as it is written, teaches that the Sabbath was coeval with the creation, appointed for all mankind through all time, and intended to be for a memorial of the creation of the world that now is. Indisputable as this appears to be, the Jews in general do not so understand the passage.

Rabbi Solomon Yarkhi says in his commentary that God sanctified the seventh day, and blessed it with manna, because on all the other days of the week an omer of bread came down to the Israelites for each person, but on the sixth day double; and the seventh He sanctified by manna, inasmuch as on that day it did not come down. This text, therefore, is written with reference to the future. Aben Ezra says nothing of the kind, but understands the blessing to consist in vigour and fecundity imparted to the creatures. Both agree in regarding the Sabbath as a gift to the Israelites only, and they date the gift from Sinai. We would not charge the Jews with a wilful conspiracy to arrogate to themselves alone the honour and blessings of the day, but would attribute their almost unanimous departure from the obvious meaning of the sacred text to a tacit understanding that the benefits of Divine revelation were bestowed on the Hebrews exclusively by inheritance from their fathers. That persuasion led them to imagine that some sentences in the prophetic books expressly marked the Sabbath as the sign of a covenant with the God of Abraham, from which the Gentiles were excluded, and ever would be, excepting those who might be admitted, by circumcision, into the congregation of the Lord's people. Those passages will come under review in due course, and.

the fact that many have been so far misled by Jews as to consider the Sabbath a Mosaic institution is all that needs be noticed now.

Let us suppose, for a moment, that the Sabbath had not been appointed when time began, but deferred until the Deluge, or the deliverance out of Egypt, or the Resurrection of Christ. In that case, the whole tenor of sacred history and doctrine must have been different from what it is.

The faith of the Old Testament is clear beyond the possibility of mistake. From the first line to the last the sacred writers teach that there is but one God, and He not an energy or a myth, but an infinite and eternal Spirit. His attributes are as himself, infinite, eternal, and immutable. They extol his wisdom, his holiness, his love. He is the Creator of all men and of all things—the God and Father of all mankind. There is no evil in his nature to counteract his goodness. He is light, and in him there is no darkness at all. The gods of the heathen are lies, abomination, and vanity, and they who trust in them are like unto them. He is judge of the whole earth, and all nations will have to stand at his bar. Clear and impressive as this truth is, it is not self-conservative. Right faith does not, like fine gold, preserve itself by its own purity, but must be held fast by those who have it.

The one God, living and true, dwelleth in thick darkness. Except that in vision He sometimes appeared to holy men, the world saw him not. Prophetic visions, although made known far and wide, were seen but by few, and that rarely. His works were indeed stupendous, and men shrank with dread from his presence as He passed by in the whirlwind, or as He rended the rocks. Men did indeed fear him, but they soon shook off the fear if they could but forget what caused it. So the tribes of Canaan, and Egypt, and the East fled from the armies of his people, and even his own people were prone to idolatry, and cast his laws behind their back.

It may be said that the works of God were sufficient to remind and even to instruct them of his goodness and power; but instead of perceiving God in his creatures, they worshipped the creatures instead of worshipping him, changing the glory of the incorruptible God into images made like unto corruptible man, and to birds, and four-footed beasts, and creeping things. "They changed the truth of God into a lie, and worshipped and served the creature more than the Creator, who is blessed for ever." This is no more than was to be expected during the ages that elapsed between the expulsion from Paradise and the call of Abraham, before a people was separated from the Gentiles or a system of worship established and a law given. Men would have become Atheists altogether unless some means had been provided for keeping up the memory of that God whom the progenitors of mankind knew.

The means provided, if fitly used, would have proved sufficient. The appropriation of one day in seven, when men's ordinary avocations were set aside, that then they might be taught his truth, and enabled to unite in his worship, was amply sufficient, and must have produced some good effect. Some, no doubt, kept the Sabbath, even in the worst times, and around that everlasting ordinance were gathered the sanctities of this life, and preparatives for the life that was to come.

CHAPTER II.

THE SABBATH BEFORE THE FLOOD.

Nothing remains of the history of the world from the expulsion of our first parents from the Garden of Eden to the Deluge, except the fourth, fifth, and sixth chapters of the Book of Genesis. These chapters are short, and from them the whole of the fifth must be deducted, as it contains nothing more than a genealogy, which does not serve our present purpose. The residue of historical notices is but forty-six verses. In these few verses there is nothing in relation to the religious state of the world to indicate that the Sabbath was set aside any more than that it was faithfully observed. It might have been kept as a secular holiday; and if there were anything to show that it was so kept, and no more, that would go some way to account for the utter corruption of society. "God saw that the wickedness of "man was great in the earth, and that every imagination of "the thoughts of his heart was only evil continually. And "it repented the Lord that He had made man on the earth, "and it grieved him at his heart." (Gen. vi. 5—6.) In such a state of human society there might be days of so-called pleasure, but there could not be days of holy rest.

One man, however, Noah, was honourably distinguished, and excepted from the general condemnation. It will be remarkable if we find in the history of himself and his family any distinct trace of religious observance of the seventh day. From the expulsion to the Deluge, according to the Ussherian chronology, was 1655 years, a very long period of moral darkness, and, for the most part, shameless impiety.

In those two chapters of Genesis, not only is the Sabbath not once mentioned, but there is not any reference to sacrifice, nor to any other religious observance. We will therefore include the narrative of the Deluge, and so enlarge the field of research by beginning at Gen. ii. 8, and ending at Gen. ix. 29. We search again, and find some trace of the division of time by weeks. There is no reason in nature for such a division, which never could have been if the primitive way of depending on the lights set in the heavens for signs and for seasons, for days and for years, were alone followed. Sight, not science, was trusted for temporal computation. Day, month, and year were natural divisions, and the counting of weeks was independent, not meant for the measurement of time, but appointed for a strictly moral reason. For a moral reason only would men count weeks; and if we find that Noah so counted, we ascertain that, notwithstanding the prevalent wickedness, and without any natural reason for marking the seventh day, which there is no evidence to show that heathens in general have done, Noah kept it holy. Now let us examine.

Gen. vii. 4. "*Yet seven days,*" said the Lord to Noah, "and I will cause it to rain upon the earth forty days and "forty nights."

vii. 10. "And it came to pass, after seven days," or rather *on the seventh day,* לְשִׁבְעַת הַיָּמִים, "that the waters of the flood "were upon the earth."

viii. 6, 7. "And it came to pass at the end" (but the Hebrew says, *after the end,* מִקֵּץ) "of forty days, that Noah "opened the window of the ark which he had made: and he "sent forth a raven." Including the seventh day, on which the rain began (vii. 10), the forty days ended on the day before the sixth seventh day, and therefore the sixth seventh day was *after* the end of forty days. "*Also* he sent forth a dove," at the same time with the raven, but while the raven "went "forth to and fro," the dove returned at once to the ark, because she "found no rest for the sole of her foot."

viii. 10, 11. "And he stayed *yet other seven days;* and again "he sent forth the dove out of the ark; and the dove came "in to him in the evening," with an olive leaf in her mouth.

viii. 12. "And he stayed *yet other seven days;* and sent "forth the dove; which returned not again unto him any more."

This exhibits six successive notations of weeks, the second and third of them clearly marking an interval of six weeks. Noah had built the ark under a Divine command, and at length, when the time came for it to be made use of, the warning was given that in seven days thence the deluge would begin. A full week was allowed for preparation, and for the great embarkation of the Patriarch and his family, with the animals to be preserved. Six weeks passed. Seven Sabbaths were counted since the windows of the ark were closed upon him, and then, according to the promise, the rain had ceased. Three times he sought to ascertain the state of the lands around; *first*, on the sixth Sabbath day after the Deluge began, the mountain-tops appeared, the loftiest heights of Ararat rising above the flood. The *second* time he sent forth the dove again on the Sabbath-day, still seeking for a token of deliverance. The *third* time, again on a Sabbath-day, he did the like. This time the dove brought back the olive-leaf, signal of restoration. Then the Patriarch was satisfied, and made no more anxious inquiries, but waited submissively until the Lord bade them all come out upon dry land again.

What shall we call those steadily-recurring seven days, if they were not Sabbath-days? So is the history of the father of the second world marked by signal evidences of faith. He had persevered through a hundred and twenty years in building an ark of precious wood for the saving of his house. He had held communion with God, who taught him how to build. He had continued in patient obedience, and, no doubt, humble prayer. This perfect man, with scrupulous punctuality, honoured the sacred day, and thus made even the ordinary action of looking out over that destroying ocean, for a mountain peak or for an island hill, a sacred act. Such an act must have been shared with his wife, their sons, and their sons' wives, eight persons looking heavenward for help, and perhaps raising a hymn of adoration, or offering an earnest prayer. Here, then, is evidence of Sabbaths kept during the Deluge, or at least, of Sabbath-days counted. This implies the like in the time of Noah before the Deluge, and the evidence is too distinct to be surrendered.

But we have yet to take another note.

It was on the first day of the first month of the six hundred and first year of Noah's life—just his birthday after completing the sixth century—that he removed the covering of the ark, looked out, and from the mountain-side saw that the earth was dry and the mists were clearing away to the vast horizon. But the land was bare as yet. On the twenty-seventh day of the second month, the lower lands being dried and blooming, God called him forth. Allowing twenty-nine days for the lunar month, here are fifty-six days counted—just eight weeks again! This makes us almost sure that the welcome sacrifice and the covenant of ever-during mercy, whereof the rainbow was the beauteous token, were the solemnities of the first Sabbath of the second world. So did that rejoicing family rest, after long trial, from the tossing of the solitary, shoreless ocean, where there was not one friendly ship that they could hail, nor so much as a haven of destination before them, or a port of refuge.

CHAPTER III.

FROM THE DELUGE TO THE EXODE.

DURING an interval of nearly one thousand years, between the entrance of Noah into the ark and the encampment of Moses and his Israelites in the Arabian wilderness, there is no mention of the Sabbath. So long silence cannot be noted without awakening surprise.

When the Creator finished his glorious work, and placed man in an abode of happiness, innocent and rejoicing, a day of holy rest, a day sanctified with God's manifested presence and communion, such blessedness was in perfect agreement with every antecedent, and with the high object of man's existence. But it was far different after the infliction of God's wrath on a wicked world, when eight persons were cast upon the wreck, with no vision of God, most of them with little knowledge, the aged head of the family betrayed into intemperance, the three sons very soon divided, each leading his family apart from the others, the scanty population eventually dispersed wide over the neglected lands, with one language indeed, but without laws, except the mere law of nature, and a conscience deadened by indifference and selfishness. Sparse and barbaric settlements, with no priesthood nor any written code civil or sacred, but a dim and dying tradition of truths but imperfectly remembered at the first, could not be expected to act with the well concerted regularity necessary for keeping holy in their petty communities one Sabbath-day common to all the race.

But even if they were not so thinly scattered, nor so rude, nor so forgetful as I have now supposed, they were about two hundred years without a history, and under a veil of impenetrable obscurity, which hid them from the knowledge of their posterity, and makes it impossible for us to conjecture with any shadow of probability what they did, or what they did not do. But we will venture to set them down as irreligious, or as knowing so little of the fundamental truths of revelation as not to show much evidence of such knowledge when they first appear upon the field of history.

Here we find them, endeavouring to build Babylon, the city where they hope to dwell together, or at least establish a strong metropolis, and raising the tower up which to climb in the event of a second deluge. They were unmindful of the promise that there should not be a second deluge. They were heedless of the sign in the cloud. What wonder, then, if they were equally forgetful and heedless as to the Sabbath appointed to be kept in memory of the Creation. But their heedlessness did not cancel the command nor obliterate the promise. He who has kept the one does not fail to enforce the other. The confusion of tongues and the dispersion of the Babel builders delayed the establishment of human society, which then had to begin again under new conditions, retarded for long time by the isolation of the several families of mankind, differing in language perhaps more than in descent.

Still, in the good providence of God, there does appear to be some shadow, at least, of an observance ancient as time itself. Perhaps before the call of Abraham, Job offered a seventh sacrifice, but whether it was offered in consideration of the seventh son, or on the seventh day, is a question. That each son had his feast punctually on the next day after one of his brothers, is not certain, and perhaps it was not possible. We cannot, therefore, surely read that Job's feasts were held every day without intermission, or, even if they were, that the arrangement was made with adaptation to the Sabbath.

The arrangement was liable to disturbance by a thousand accidents, and if once put out of order, the Sabbath-count was lost. (Job i. 1—5.) Nothing can be made of this.

After the call of Abraham, there is at least the appearance of a Sabbath. Jacob kept his wedding-feast for seven days. (Gen. xxix. 27.) Joseph and his brethren made a solemn mourning for their father Jacob seven days. (Gen. l. 10.) Samson in Philistia feasted at his wedding seven days. (Judges xiv. 12.) Religious observance became all those occasions, and we at least find a trace of Sabbatic memory.

During the wanderings of the Patriarchs it would be too much to expect a revival of the primitive Sabbath without an express Divine command. Such command there was not. But the chosen people were as yet but nomads; and as the Sabbath had not been made for a single family or tribe, but for all mankind, a solemn reappointment of it would not probably be made in an encampment of Abraham's trained servants, or among the wandering herdsmen of Jacob or of Esau, much less among the Hebrew slaves in Egypt. Such a reappointment was indeed made with the highest solemnity, not in Goshen, but east of the Red Sea, as soon as the liberated slaves found themselves with Moses and Aaron at their head, and the Lord God of Hosts in the midst of them.

I doubt if a slave population ever has duly kept a Sabbath. Even the comparatively mild form of slavery which I knew in an English colony a few years before our national emancipation, under the meliorating influence of Christianity and the watchful eye of British philanthropy, did not allow the negro to take Sabbath-rest beyond a very imperfect respite once a fortnight. He was always at his master's mercy. Much less would the Egyptian taskmasters exempt their slaves from labour in order that they might fulfil a religious duty. It was on this very account that Moses and his brother were sent to demand liberty for them to go into the wilderness to sacrifice to the Lord their God. Even Moses, with all his zeal for his people—for they could not yet be called a nation—did not know the name of the God of their fathers; yet that primeval name had been pronounced by Eve, was revealed again to Abraham, and perpetuated until Jacob, who used it on his death-bed, at least in prayer.

If, then, the Sabbath is almost half forgotten among ourselves, and altogether desecrated in some professedly Protestant countries, we could hardly expect to hear that the Egyptians would suffer their poor slaves to honour it, even if it were not then unknown, which is most probable.

CHAPTER IV.

THE SABBATH LAW NOT LEVITICAL.

When it pleased the Lord to send his servants into Egypt to bring their brethren out of bondage, He did not instruct them to require the performance of any act of worship. Moses and Aaron offered no sacrifice. Until the night of the Passover there is no religious solemnity mentioned except the prayers of Moses for Pharaoh, and invocations attending the wonders which God wrought in vengeance upon the oppressor of his people. Not a child was circumcised. The first thing done was to demand their liberty; the second was to enforce the demand. They were then brought out with a mighty hand and outstretched arm, marching from Goshen to the Red Sea, and across the sea-bed to the Arabian shore. After singing a song of triumph*, they proceeded

---

* In that song of triumph there were intimations of an established state of things not yet existing—a state absolutely necessary for the full observance of an essentially *social law*, as is that of the Sabbath, which must be sustained by a constitution of society with which it can be in practical agreement. In prophetic anticipation of such a condition of society, Moses sang—"The Lord . . . is my God, and I will "prepare him *an habitation;* my father's God, and I will exalt him. " . . . Thou hast guided (thy people) in thy strength unto thy *holy* "*habitation*. . . Thou shalt bring them in, and plant them in the "mountain of thine *inheritance*, in the place, O Lord, which Thou hast "made *for thee to dwell in, in the Sanctuary*, O Lord, which thy hands "have established." (Exod. xv. 2. 13. 17.) In that place they could secure for themselves Sabbatic rest and quiet, which was not possible in Egypt, nor would be possible in any land of their captivity without the favour of strangers. But it would be made possible wherever the people of the country acknowledged the Lord to be their God.

inland, and then began a new dispensation of God's gracious government.

"All the congregation of the children of Israel came unto the wilderness of Sin, which is between Elim and Sinai, on the fifteenth day of the second month after their departing out of the land of Egypt." (Exod. xvi. 1.) There they began to suffer want of food, and in horror of impending famine murmured against Moses and Aaron. "Then said the Lord unto Moses, Behold, I will rain bread from heaven for you; and the people shall go out and gather a certain rate every day, that I may prove them, whether they will walk in my law, or no." For they had not yet been brought under God's law, and the proof of their willingness to walk in it would be that "on the sixth day" they should prepare that which they brought in, and it should be twice as much as they gathered daily (v. 4, 5). During five days of disquiet they ate quails in the evenings, and manna in the mornings, "and on the sixth day they gathered twice as much" of this heaven-sent bread in the morning. "And all the rulers of the congregation came and told Moses. And he said unto them, This is that which the Lord hath said, to-morrow is the rest of the holy Sabbath unto the Lord: bake that which ye will bake to-day, and seethe that ye will seethe; and that which remaineth over lay up for you to be kept until the morning. And they laid it up till the morning, as Moses bade: and it did not stink, neither was there any worm therein. And Moses said, Eat that to-day; for to-day is a Sabbath unto the Lord: to-day ye shall not find it in the field. Six days ye shall gather it; but on the seventh day, which is the Sabbath, in it there shall be none" (v. 22. to 26.) Some of the people notwithstanding went out to gather on the Sabbath-day, and were rebuked for disobedience. "So the people rested."

From the day when Moses was commanded so to instruct the people, until the day when he came down from the mountain with the tables of the Decalogue, was certainly more than two months, probably not less than three. At its first announcement the Sabbath was not described as of new appointment, but simply named as *the Sabbath* of the Lord. The allusion is emphatic. The earliest record is preserved by the hand of Moses himself. There cannot be any misapprehension. The words of the commandment inscribed on the stone expressly declare the same, and those words we now proceed to examine, endeavouring to ascertain how much they require, and whether they contain or imply any limitation to the Hebrews only.

The words of the fourth commandment (Exod. xx. 8—11) are so familiar in every household, that it cannot be necessary to repeat them here at length.

They were not commanded to remember the *seventh day*, for then it would have been needful to specify a day at which the counting should begin—whether from the covenant with Noah, or from the going into the Ark, or from the day when God ceased from the creation, or the day when Moses led them out from Goshen, or some other day that might be chosen. But such calculations are sometimes impossible, difficult at best, often doubtful, and the more doubtful or disputable, the more excusable is failure of conformity to the observance. Remote calculations were avoided. It was said on the eve of the first day of rest, "To-morrow is the Sab-"bath of the Lord," and after each seventh day had been regularly set apart, the double supply of manna being gathered on the day preceding, and the weekly rest well established it was written on the table of stone, *Remember the day of the Sabbath*, אֶת־יוֹם הַשַּׁבָּת; that is to say, the day on which the Sabbath is kept. The *rest* is distinct from the *day*. The day is to be kept holy for the sake of the rest thereon appointed, but the rest is not to be taken for the sake of the day. The first Sabbath-day in the wilderness was in no sense the seventh from the Sabbath-day before it. Ages, not days, had passed away without a Sabbath. That Sabbath-day had relation only to the week of manna, just as the first of all Sabbath-days had relation only to the week of creation, of which it was the day of sanctification and blessing. Rest thus hallowed is truly Sabbatic, which mere cessation from labour would not be. A day of resting for the sake of recreation only, could not, with any shadow of propriety, be called " the Sabbath of the Lord thy God."

The Hebrews in the wilderness were to *remember* the day not only on its return, but all the week through. They were to remember it, first, in the diligent discharge of each day's duty, that they might be able to rest without distraction of care, or condemnation because of negligence, which implies dishonesty and sin, when the seventh day came. They were to remember the Sabbath, secondly, by habitual provision during the six days for its due observance on the seventh. The prospect of a rational, man-like, and holy rest would encourage them to daily industry. Sabbath was thus made subservient to the ordinary discipline of life.

They were to *sanctify* the day when it came. This could not be done by mere suspension of labour, for that would be nothing more than idleness, which is the surest inlet to vice; but as the Lord himself had sanctified it so should they. A practical sanctification was to be conducted with reference to God, and this pre-supposes some kind of religious observance. Experience has taught us that this, more than anything else, makes the Sabbath a delight; whereas a constrained cessation, a sudden check interrupting every movement of common life, he dropping anchor for twenty-four hours when just in sight of harbour, and forbidding even a wish to step on shore after having watchfully caught even the lightest breeze, and spared no effort to accomplish the six days' toil, would have been to tantalize rather than reward.

God's blessing on the parents of mankind in Paradise on the first day of their life must have impressed the conscience of the first human family; and the command now so solemnly delivered to a ransomed nation by the very voice of God their Saviour, must have been unspeakably more significant to all who heard it, than a bald injunction to be silent and still until the next sun rose. Rather were they to look on Heaven, Earth, and Sea, with all that in them is—to observe the grandeur of the desert, the solemnity of the sky-encircled ocean, the glory of Lebanon and the beauty of Carmel, all the abundance of their harvests, everything that could be seen or thought on as dear to man and acceptable to God, a universe of beauty and goodness all combining to give impulse to honest industry; and God's favour above the whole crowning their earthly joys with heavenly delight.

Even on the day of rest there was much to be done, if men would avoid doing then what God forbids. The words of the commandment are clear enough, if correctly read: "*Thou shalt not do any of thy business.*" לֹא־תַעֲשֶׂה כָל־מְלַאכְתֶּךָ. For מְלָאכָה is very different from עֲבוֹדָה; it is one's own business, not labour in the service of another, whether servitude to man or worship to God. The word used in the commandment denotes the business which one can order for himself— daily occupation—the vocation which is pursued under a sense of responsibility, yet with a consciousness of freedom. It may be the business of the lawyer, the merchant, the tradesman, the artificer. It may be the service of the free labourer or freely hired servant. There is a daily business which may be distinguished from what is emergent or necessary without regard of days, all that may be done in six days and suspended on the seventh. Necessity, if it be not artificial, and charity are liabilities of life that, unlike the fabled Sabbatic river, flow every day and every night without respect of seasons. They are no man's *business*, but they are every man's doom or duty. Men and angels are alike bound to this perpetual ministration of succour to the afflicted, healing to the sick, rescue to the imperilled. These holy services are not rendered so much to man as to God, services from which God has not excused us, but which are ever falling into arrear, and, therefore, He allots a day every week in which we may pay up the arrears in blessings to those around us, and not less to ourselves, if rightly done. They differ much from the common transactions of mankind among themselves, done for themselves, and done in their own way, but limited within six days of the seven, and finished then.

When speaking of the Christian Sabbath I shall have more to say, but this is here said in order to explain, as clearly as I can, the language of the commandment. While the Hebrews were in Egypt they had no freemen's *business*, מלאבה; it was all עבדה, involuntary, servile *drudgery*. The slaves are now emancipated. They have come over into the wilderness that they may worship the God of their fathers. Now they have to transact the business of men. They are free from Pharaoh, and are set free that they may be as much in happy subjection to God's law as Adam in Eden or Noah in the Ark. To have renewed the Sabbath to them in Egypt would have been to draw down Pharaoh's vengeance on themselves for letting the slaves from their labours. Therefore, the slaves were brought out of Egypt, and, as no master now stands between them and God, they are summoned to perform the duties and enjoy the rights of men.

Now they will be masters, having servants of their own.

They will be a nation, lords over their own territory, having strangers within their gates; but even so they must not be tyrants, nor exact from those servants what belongs to the Lord of all. The man-servant and the maid-servant are to rest as well as the master and mistress; the Gentile as well as the Israelite. The conditions of servitude should here be noted. A Hebrew might sell himself to a Hebrew purchaser for six years, and when the seventh year came, he might either go free or, by voluntary submission, remain servant for life. In that case his ear was bored, and, of his own free will, he chose a life-long servitude with maintenance at his master's cost, and no care for himself. Prisoners of war, too, were slaves, and might be kept in slavery for life, always protected under humane laws which signally elevated the civil law of the Mosaic dispensation above the codes of all contemporaneous nations. There were, indeed, certain condemned tribes whom the Israelites were required to extirpate, but even the extirpation of those savages was the most humane measure that could be taken in order to assure the safety of the inhabitants in general. The Hebrews might buy heathens for slaves, but the slaves were immediately taken under the protection of special statutes, and exempted from labour on the Sabbath-day. The heathen stranger in a Hebrew town enjoyed his liberty, so long as he obeyed the laws.

The inclusion, then, of strangers and servants, under one common obligation for the sake of a common benefit, proves that heathens were not overlooked by the Divine Legislator; but in course of time the doctrine that Sabbath was given for the children of Jacob only, and that the Gentiles were utterly excluded from its benefits, took possession of the Israelitish mind.

The tender mercy which is over all the works of God, and takes within its view the meanest creatures, provided that cattle also should rest. The beast of burden, brought under the yoke for man, is to be compensated by having a share with his master in the Sabbath-rest.

With regard to the word *stranger*, גֵר, we must note that it cannot be fairly interpreted to mean a proselyte, much less a proselyte incorporated with the congregation by circumcision. The Septuagint does indeed apply this meaning to the word, or rather adds it to the proper translation of the word, by the expedient of a paraphrase. That version has it—"thy ox, and thy ass, and all thy cattle, and the "proselyte that is a stranger with thee." But ox, ass, and proselyte, are all interpolated. The Talmudists, it is true, use the word גֵר for proselyte, but I believe it is not so used anywhere in the Old Testament, and neither the Samaritan Hebrew Text nor the Targum of Onkelos lends the least support to such a provision, nor affords any countenance to those who would wish to make it appear that the Sabbath is a Mosaic, or as they yet more foolishly say, a Jewish institution.

The commandment closes with an explicit recital of the original appointment. "For in six days the Lord made "heaven and earth, the sea, and all that in them is, and rested "the seventh day; wherefore the Lord blessed the Sabbath "day, and hallowed it."

It is not enough to say that the Sabbath law was revived in the wilderness, and that the original precept was embodied in the law delivered to Moses in Mount Sinai. Moses was careful to describe the course of events with great distinctness in that part of his history; and in order to estimate aright the relation of each law to the entire code, and to ascertain the reason of each, the Mosaic narrative must be carefully examined.

We have already observed that the obligation to cease

from labour on the seventh day was inculcated by Divine command when the manna was given, some months before the Israelites encamped before Mount Sinai, and waited there to receive, for the first time, a code of laws for their government.

After the cloud, which indicated the presence of the Lord, had rested on the mountain for some days, and Moses was instructed that the people were not to come up the mountain, nor even approach beyond the bounds that were to be set, He called Moses into his presence, and *spake* to him the *Ten Words*, that is to say, the Ten Commandments. The people " saw the thunderings and the lightnings, and the noise of the " trumpet, and the mountain smoking, and when the people " saw it they removed and stood afar off." Moses then drew near unto the thick darkness where God was, and received some instruction concerning the first principles of Divine worship, and those relative duties which are bounden on all human society. The language in which those instructions were delivered was indeed suitable to their condition at the time, yet the terms were general, and the duties enjoined proper for men of any nation or country in the world—bating only as much as related to sacrifice, which had indeed been offered almost from the beginning of time, and some provisions against superstitious and idolatrous customs to be from that time abandoned. The Lord also promised to send an angel with Moses to keep him and the people by the way, to bring them to the promised land, and prosper them there. The last promise, however, was limited most expressly by the condition that they should render him faithful service, with undivided worship and unreserved obedience.

Moses then came down from the mountain, told the people all the words of the Lord, received their promise that they would do all things which the Lord had said, wrote in a book all that had been delivered to him, and by him repeated to the people, erected an altar without delay, and therewith twelve pillars according to the twelve tribes of Israel, offered burnt offerings, sacrificed peace-offerings of oxen unto the Lord, " and took the book of the covenant, and read in the audience " of the people; and they said, All that the Lord hath said " will we do, and be obedient. And Moses took the blood " and sprinkled it on the people, and said, Behold the blood " of the covenant which the Lord hath made with you con- " cerning these words."

This describes, in few words, long and most careful preparation; not one continuous proceeding, but many successive acts, well devised and deliberately executed, in pursuance of explicit instructions from the Lord. The people were fully informed, and that work of preliminary instruction could not have been dispatched in haste. The whole was closed with high solemnity. All the people gave assent, not tacit but express. They professed themselves resolved to abandon idolatry, and no doubt accompanied that profession with marks of earnestness which satisfied their captain that they were sincere.

Being thus assured, Moses, Aaron, Nadab, and Abihu, with seventy of the elders of Israel, in obedience to a summons from the Lord, went up into the mountain, and " saw " the God of Israel," which gave those elders full certainty that he had indeed received by Divine revelation the commands which he delivered to the people.

Yet again the Lord called Moses up into the mountain, who went, attended by Joshua his servant, leaving the elders in the camp, with Aaron and Hur at their head, to act for him in his absence.

" A cloud covered the mount. The glory of the Lord " abode upon Mount Sinai, and the cloud covered it six days: " and the seventh day He called unto Moses out of the midst "of the cloud. And the sight of the glory of the Lord was "like devouring fire on the top of the mount in the eyes of "the children of Israel." (Exod. xxiv. 15—17.) Thus did the Lord visibly mark the week—six days within the cloud, the seventh by calling his servant into his immediate presence. Thus being summoned, Moses went alone within the cloud. There he received "tables of stone, and a law, and command-"ments, which the Lord had written."

It was then that he remained forty days and forty nights, receiving full instruction in the ceremonial law, and the entire system of government that should be from that time administered. There he kept Sabbath with the Lord at the beginning of those days.

At the end of those forty days he came down from the mountain, carrying with him "two tables of testimony, tables "of stone, written with the finger of God." The reader will remember how Moses perceived, as he approached the camp, that the people, led by his brother Aaron, were worshipping a golden calf, and how, in an agony of indignant horror, he dashed the tablets to the ground, and broke them to pieces. His anger, the repentance of the people, the plague that followed, and Moses' intercession on their behalf, need not be related here.

Again, Moses is on the mount in the presence of the Lord, and is assured of pardon and reconciliation for the people. As commanded, he has hewed two tables of stone in place of those which are broken. Having received further communications of the Divine will, again he "was there with the "Lord forty days and forty nights, and did neither eat bread "nor drink water; and he wrote upon the tables the words "of the covenant, the ten commandments." There was much else that Moses wrote, but this additional writing was totally distinct. It was the record of what the Lord had spoken first of all, and, as it is said in the Book of Deuteronomy, *he added no more*. These commandments, and these alone, were the substance of the *covenant* into which the people had entered with sacrifice long before the Mosaic Law or Levitical Ritual was given. Furthermore, we observe that no part of that covenant was made more prominent than the fourth commandment; for when Moses came down from Mount Sinai, after being with the Lord a second time for forty days and forty nights, he did not, as before, recite the whole Decalogue, although he brought it with him on the marble, but said, " These are the words which the Lord hath " commanded, that ye should do them. Six days shall work " be done, but on the seventh day there shall be to you an " holy day, a Sabbath of rest unto the Lord: whosoever " doth work therein shall be put to death. Ye shall kindle " no fire throughout your habitations upon the Sabbath day." (Exod. xxxv. 1—3.) Thus was the Sabbath made the *sign* between God and his people—sign of the covenant. To break the Sabbath was to break the covenant, and this accounts for the severity of the law.

Thus briefly I endeavour to give a summary of the sacred narrative, but recommend a careful perusal of the text itself, from Exod. xx. 1 to xxxv. 3. That will show that although the body of laws by which the Israelites were to be governed under the Mosaic dispensation, as it is fitly called, was fully delivered to Moses, and the fundamental code of moral law known as the Decalogue was also given to Moses; the two were held totally distinct. Spoken by the Lord at first, without the admission of any other precepts on the tables of stone, it alone was made the substance of a solemn covenant before the ceremonial law was given. After it, not before nor with it, the priesthood was appointed, and the Levitical ceremonial of worship. This ritual, however, was no part of God's covenant.

One thing more is remarkable, as regards the Sabbatic statute, and it is this, that on the renewal of the broken covenant that only was recited to the people with the addition of the ultimate penalty for the offence of breaking it. Like the tree of life in Paradise, the Sabbath is made the signal of communion between God and man. Yet, most strangely, some men would have us to believe that Christianity cancels this one commandment of the ten as being Jewish and obsolete. Moses, while yet the rays of heavenly light were sparkling in his brow, is fancied to have had less of spiritual discernment than distinguishes these latter-day divines.

Yet there is a word more to be said concerning a point on which I have touched above, but not exhausted.

Gentile strangers, not proselytes but heathens, when within the gates of the Israelite, were permitted, and even bound, to keep the Sabbath. They were fully exempted from their ordinary occupations, and were not to work for the Hebrew, who could not compel even his own heathen slave to do it for him on that day, any more than his heathen visitor. But it is equally clear that the same heathen, whether servant, guest, or friend, could not be permitted to share with him a Passover supper, nor to participate in the observance of the Feast of Tabernacles, nor any other feast, nor in any sacrifice. What then does this exception mean, except it be that the sacrifices, the feasts and the fasts are all for the Israelites alone, but that the Sabbath is for all the world? And why were the Mosaic priesthood and ritual kept out of sight in the covenant so solemnly made with the Israelites before the Law, except because the truths and relations set forth in the Decalogue are those which may be the link of communion between God and man, irrespective of that law?

Another fact demands attention here. A mixed multitude

came out of Egypt with the Israelites, and other Gentiles were continually mingling with them during the forty years' pilgrimage. None of them, so long as he remained uncircumcised, was admitted into the congregation of the Lord; yet every one of them was obliged to keep the Sabbath. During the days of wonder that we have now recounted, when the visible glory rested on Mount Sinai, they were not recognized in any of the great solemnities, yet they, their wives, and their children, rested every Sabbath. Sabbath rest was as free to them as daily manna, of which their portion on the sixth day was double as much as any other. There was not yet a person in existence answering to the modern description of "Jew," much less a Jewish Sabbath. No rabbi yet breathed to preach that the Gentile servant might work on the Sabbath to minister to his Hebrew master's luxury. The mixed multitude was not marched out of camp that the Ten Commandments might be recited to the twelve tribes. It would have been contrary to the will of God, to sound reason, and to wise policy. Had the heathen been exempted from obedience to any one of the Ten Commandments there would have been sad work in camp. They were, as they still are, a moral code of universal obligation—a covenant bond for uniting man to God, for the acknowledgment of God's universal authority; and if even the heathen will but acknowledge this, they are at once brought within the circle of redeeming mercy by penitential faith in Christ. The Sabbath law and Sabbath blessing are alike for Jew and Gentile, as much as are the common sunshine and the common shower.

Yet again: the Sabbath was above the feasts. The feasts were movable, the Sabbaths fixed. The feasts followed with the changing moons, having relation to mundane seasons. The Sabbath-day is known on its return without any question, but not so the new moon if the sky is overcast, or the hour unfavourable for observation. An exact calculation of the time necessary to complete the solar year by the addition of another lunar month, and again to make the cycle good by a further addition or delay to restore the order of time and season, was always difficult, if not impossible, until science overcame the difficulty. But nothing is more simple than to count seven suns and so make the Sabbath sure. From the foundation of the world God had appointed this to be done, and, therefore, when Moses was instructed to promulgate a Law for his chosen people, the Sabbath-day was set before all festivals, and its return made independent of them all. It began before them; it continued when their due observance became impossible; it remained when they were set aside.

So remote from the common course of human experience was the current of affairs during the Arabian pilgrimage that it scarcely enters into our thoughts to attempt any conception of what a Sabbath-keeping might have been when the tribes of Israel lay encamped in the wâdys of the desert. No fires were to be lit, no food cooked, no common work done. The extent of this last prohibition has been considered above; and with regard to the preparation of food we may observe that in the climate of Stony Arabia fires may be dispensed with at almost any time without much inconvenience. During their pilgrimage the Israelites were under special guidance and provision, and sheltered from the inclemencies of weather which would have been insupportable without such protection.

The penalty of death was pronounced against any wilful breach of this commandment; first, for the reason already assigned that to keep the Sabbath was a condition of the covenant, of which the Sabbath was the sign; and also for other obvious reasons. On one occasion the penalty was actually inflicted, but not on any other, so far as is recorded. In spite of the solemn prohibition a man went out of camp to gather sticks, and having singly and stubbornly committed an outrage against the authority of the God of Israel, he suffered death for the "presumptuous sin." Had that first open and insolent transgressor been allowed impunity, the law would soon have been set at nought by all the people, and the consequences of lawlessness would have been fearful indeed. Those hundreds of thousands of newly-emancipated slaves could only be protected against themselves by the firm administration of a stern and unflinching justice. There was no armed force to keep them in check, no system of human government that could be trusted; nor can we gather from the history that they had yet the power of discerning steadily between right and wrong, or that any appeal to conscience or to reason would have restrained them in a moment of discontent or passion. Nothing less than an unequivocal display of avenging power would subdue their stubbornness, and even that did not suffice for long.

Soon as they saw the only alternative, death or submission, they kept the Sabbath. How they kept it is not known, and perhaps there is not any indication sufficient to sustain a conjecture. We only know that the din of work was hushed. On entering into the Sabbath-hour at sunset the smoke of the camp-fires passed off, and the glare slowly diminished; but although fires might not now be kindled, there was nothing to hinder the flame of night-fire or of night-lamp, lit before sundown, from being kept up if needed. The pillar of heavenly fire, ever burning, no doubt shed its mild light over the watching or the slumbering thousands, no less in season than the playful *aurora borealis* that in the long arctic nights provides a secondary day. On the dawn of the desert Sabbath no smoke mingled with the pure morning air, neither did the unclouded burning sun distress, for the ever-present canopy of sacred cloud screened them from its fierceness.

Whether with patriarchal prayers, or with exultant hymns like that triumphal song chanted on the sea-shore by Aaron and Miriam and caught up by the ransomed myriads, or with holy teaching and admonition by the elders in the midst of their tribes, we cannot say. We presume to believe that in some way suitable and sufficient the day was hallowed. The heathen camp follower was not suffered to disturb the quiet. Yet who can say that the wild Ishmaelite, or the fierce Amalekite or Moabite, would not sometimes venture to approach—unless the fear and dread of Israel's God kept such away—and would wonder as, from the cleft of some distant rock, he gazed on the grandeur of so great a force in calm repose. Men of war, often seen in battle, fierce as lions in conflict, swift as eagles in pursuit, cutting down their enemies like grass of the field, were, on this day of truce, silent and immovable. As for themselves, the unbroken silence of the desert certified that no hostile enemy was near, or they would have perceived the vibration of even the far approaching march amidst those awful solitudes. Perhaps, ever and again, a wild song of praise, chastened into sweetness, would float along the valley, or be reverberated among the mountains, and as the chorus from the lips of old and young swelled like thunder, the cheerful, solemn Hallelujah, so grandly contrasted with the defiant war-whoop of other days, would convey to the listening stranger a sense of the goodness of the Hebrews' God.

Enforced observance could never be sincere, and the review of "the abominations of their fathers," which the prophet Ezekiel set before the elders of Israel, proves that they "polluted the Sabbaths of the Lord." (Ezek. xx.) But I may be permitted to doubt whether "Sabbaths," in that place, does not refer to all the sacred feasts, and not to the Sabbaths only. Of course, Sabbath-worship was no less polluted than the rest, but the manner of pollution referred to by Ezekiel appears to be the introduction of idolatrous rites, such as they had been familiar with in Egypt.

That pollution of the Sabbath by idolatry, or false worship, differs from Sabbath-breaking by prohibited labour, appears very distinctly, on careful perusal of the twentieth chapter of the Book of the Prophet Ezekiel, and other similar passages. And how far the Sabbath may not be polluted by the substitution of false worship for true, of operatic entertainment for genuine devotion, is a question worthy of most grave consideration by popular preachers of all religious denominations, mercenary proprietaries, and shallow ceremonialists. This is a topic for study, and perhaps it would be useful to try how far Sabbath-pollution may not extend into what now passes as decent, or at least allowedly attractive "services." *Worship* it cannot be truly called, but *exhibition*.

The appointment of a Sabbath of years, and a year of release, or jubilee, on every seventh Sabbatic year, was entirely Mosaic, and applied only to the Holy Land. It is not implied in any sentence or allusion of Holy Scripture before the giving of the Mosaic Law, nor has it any relation to the world at large. I have therefore avoided all mention of it here, and leave the reader to examine the twenty-fifth chapter of Leviticus and judge for himself.

CHAPTER V.

FROM THE PASSAGE OF THE JORDAN TO THE BABYLONISH CAPTIVITY.

So long as the Hebrews were on their pilgrimage, dependent for daily food or supplies direct from the hand of God, and immediately in subjection to God for both reward and punishment, an external observance of the weekly solemnity could not be avoided. But as it is not consistent with a first principle of Divine government to compel obedience, compulsion was only employed during the time when it pleased God to remove the Hebrew nation from utter subjugation to Egyptian tyranny, and gradually prepare it for a state of liberty. To this end the tribes were kept apart from all ordinary communications with their fellow-men in that most dreary wilderness, and placed under an extraordinary discipline. There, in a condition of social infancy, they were taught the first elements of revealed religion, and made in some degree familiar with the obligations of a moral law.

When due preparation had been made for celebrating Divine worship under the direction of Aaron, first High Priest, " the Lord spake unto Moses, saying, Speak unto the " children of Israel, and say unto them; Concerning the feasts " of the Lord, which ye shall proclaim to be holy convocations, " even these are my feasts. Six days shall work be done: but " the seventh day is the Sabbath of rest, an holy convoca- " tion; ye shall do no work therein: it is the Sabbath of the " Lord in all your dwellings." (Lev. xxiii. 1—3.) After the Sabbath came the feasts, distinctively so called, holy convocations, to be proclaimed in their seasons.

This may be considered as the standing regulation, and, being studied carefully, it becomes evident—

1. That the Sabbath differs from those feasts, in that it is not limited to any season of the year, but must be kept in all seasons.

2. That while a proclamation is necessary before even the appointed feast is held, every one is bound to keep the Sabbath without waiting for a proclamation.

3. But it is not inferior to any feast. No less than the most solemn festival, it is to be honoured with *a holy convocation*, מִקְרָא־קֹדֶשׁ, when the people were to be called together for a holy purpose.

4. It was not to be a mere weekly holiday, but a *Sabbath of rest*, שַׁבַּת־שַׁבָּתוֹן, a Sabbath of the Lord, consecrated to his service and honour.

5. Distance from Jerusalem, or even from the Holy Land, would not find any Israelite exempted from the Sabbath-law, nor imply an exclusion from its benefits. It should be kept *in all their* dwellings or *places of abode*, מוֹשְׁבֹתֵיכֶם, wherever their abode might be, in their own land, or in dispersion.

6. As we often have occasion to observe, every festival was distinctly Mosaic, having reference to the system of worship established under Moses, but the Sabbath was from the beginning of time.

Shortly before the death of Moses, Joshua was appointed his successor; and after this appointment, Moses, by Divine command, gave a special direction that, in addition to the daily burnt-offering of two lambs, there should be other two lambs, and two tenth deals of flour, indicating a high Sabbatic solemnity. (Num. xxviii. 9, 10.) On occasion of this proper sacrifice for the Sabbath we may suppose that the holy convocation would take place.

Moses, immediately before his death, made a solemn recapitulation of all the laws previously delivered, including the Decalogue, when he told them that God had written those words on two tables of stone, and then again the Fourth Commandment had a note of distinction given it. There was a special motive for including their servants with themselves in the repose and comfort of the day—by servants being meant Gentile servants, of course—wherefore these words were added: "And remember that thou wast a servant in the "land of Egypt, and that the Lord thy God brought thee "out thence through a mighty hand and by a stretched-out "arm: therefore the Lord thy God commanded thee to "keep the Sabbath-day." (Deut. v. 15.) Moses did not say that, therefore, God had appointed the day which was to be so kept, for that would have been to contradict what was already stated; but that therefore, it being already *appointed*, and the reason of its appointment written in marble by the finger of God, he commanded them to *keep* it, and to give to their Gentile servants what Gentile masters had denied to them—Sabbath rest.

More than four hundred years after shewbread was first placed before the Sanctuary on the Sabbath-day, to be afterwards eaten by the priests, we read of the designation of some of the sons of the Kohathites to be " over the shewbread, to " prepare it every Sabbath." This was in force in the time of Saul, when the Israelites and Philistines were at war (1 Chron. ix. 32); and we know that this Sabbath-duty continued to be performed during the reign of David. Numerous parties of Levites, who lodged within the precinct of the Temple when on duty there, entered on their duty after seven days " from time to time." (1 Chron. ix. 25.) " The King's " guard," which must have been very strong, was relieved on the Sabbath; and it was on that sacred day that Jehoiada the priest, having engaged the help of the "rulers over hundreds, "with the captains and the guard," had orders given to detain them that went forth on the Sabbath to unite with them that came in, and, being fully armed, to surround the young prince Joash, and keep the gates to prevent interruption, while they proclaimed him king, in view of restoring the worship of the Lord, and putting away idolatrous practices. (2 Kings xi. 4—16.)

It is said that a trumpet was sounded at sunset in Jerusalem to let the inhabitants know that the Sabbath was begun; and it has been conjectured that *the covert for the Sabbath* which Ahaz demolished in the Temple was built for the convenience of those who assembled for that purpose, that they might be sheltered from the weather. (2 Kings xvi. 18.)

Ushered in with solemnity, and guarded with most scrupulous care, this was in every respect the queen of days. All things were made ready for a holy convocation, and the sacred services which were to sanctify the toils of the working days began. The Priests, the Levites, and the Nethinims entered on their weekly course. The shewbread was laid upon the golden table, twelve loaves, a loaf for a tribe; for although several of the tribes worshipped apart at Bethel, none were forgotten at Jerusalem. The lambs and oblation of the day were duly offered. A great assembly crowded the courts. Devout persons came to inquire of the Lord, as appears incidentally in the narrative of the Shunammite woman. (2 Kings iv. 23.) All traffic and negotiation was suspended, as well as all manual labour—commerce as well as toil. So signally hallowed was the day, that all the week received from it a name, and men counted not so much by weeks, as the rabbis do now, but by Sabbaths. "Count seven Sabbaths," said Moses.

Yet all were not content, nor was the ideal of an unreserved sanctification to God grateful to the worldly-minded.

Whether or not, the poor were pleased to rest along with the unyoked cattle, but the rich betrayed weariness under the restraint and grudged the hours taken away from Mammon. "When will the Sabbath be gone?" they asked imperiously. "When will the Sabbath be gone, that we may sell corn, and "set forth wheat, making the ephah small, and the shekel "great, and falsifying the balances by deceit?" (Amos viii. 5, 6.) The day once consecrated to the worship of God and the refreshment of men was intended to be a delight, that rich and poor together might rejoice in it and be glad; but a prophet, burdened with a message of reproof, was heard to say of Jerusalem, speaking in the name of the Lord, "I will "cause all her mirth to cease, her feast-days, her new moons, "and her Sabbaths, and all her solemn feasts." (Hosea ii. 11.)

We glean from the historical Scriptures information concerning the external services of the Sabbath. The prophets tell us what was the spirit of the law that thus fell into contempt and desuetude.

Isaiah, who began his mission more than a century and a half before Jerusalem fell by the arms of Nebuchadnezzar, most explicitly declares what God requires of his people on the Sabbath-day. His prophecies open with an impassionate cry that God was weary of their new moons and Sabbaths, which had become an abomination to him. (Is. i. 12, 13.) At another time the same prophet acknowledges that there were yet some who kept the Sabbath from polluting it—what is meant by pollution I have already pointed out—and kept their hands from doing evil. Such persons, he says, are blessed. He testifies that the Lord has promised inestimable blessings and perpetual memory to them who so do, and not only to the circumcised descendants of Jacob, but to the sons of the stranger who join themselves to the Lord, to serve him, to love his name, to keep the Sabbath from polluting it, and to lay hold on his covenant. For there was a covenant, as this demonstrates, by which the son of the stranger could join himself to the Lord, as well as the covenant of Abraham. The Lord said, by his servant Isaiah, that he would bring the strangers to his holy mountain, and make them joyful in his house of prayer, and that that house should be called a house of prayer for all people. (Is. lvi. 3—7.) To any and every one that would turn away his foot from doing his own pleasure on God's holy day, who would call the Sabbath a delight, the holy of the Lord, honourable, and would honour him, not doing his own ways, nor finding his own pleasure, nor speaking his own words; to him the prophet was sent to promise that he should delight himself in the Lord, who would cause him to ride on the high places of the earth, and feed him with the heritage of Jacob his father, for the mouth of the Lord had spoken it. (Is. lviii. 13, 14.)

Any careful reader of the Bible, but most certainly the exact historical student who marks the course of events, their chronological order, their natural sequence, and the place of each—so far as it can be ascertained—in relation to the entire story, cannot fail to observe that as the Hebrew state decays, and civil polity and religious worship grow more and more corrupt, there is a lesser stress laid on the Mosaic ceremonial; sacrifice gives way to prayer, the pomp of ritual perishes, sincere men are encouraged to seek Divine knowledge and to cultivate brotherly communion outside the Temple.

They foresaw the great calamity as it was approaching The Temple would soon be laid in ruins; the sacrificial fire quenched; the Ark lost; the glory departed; Jerusalem a heap; princes, priests, prophets carried away into captivity. Then there were promises which we must not overlook, if we would fairly appreciate the holy institution which I am now endeavouring to trace amidst the vicissitudes of history. It was promised that when the Levitical system should be abolished the Sabbath would remain. In the last chapter of the Book of the Prophet Isaiah, where it is foretold that the Gentiles shall be gathered, and that Israelites shall go forth into the world to proclaim the glory of the Lord, these notable words are written: "As the new heavens and the "new earth, which I will make, shall remain before me, saith "the Lord, so shall your seed and your name remain. And "it shall come to pass, that from one new moon to another, "*and from one Sabbath to another, shall all flesh come to* "*worship before me, saith the Lord.*" (Is. lxvi. 22, 23.) So does the Gospel prophet sing of the seed and the name of Jacob, without the ceremonial of Levi—the coming of all flesh, without limitation of people or lineage, to worship before the Lord, without Levitical ceremonies, from moon to moon, from Sabbath to Sabbath.

When Ezekiel was himself a captive, and the "New Jeru- "salem"—understood in the Christian Scriptures to be the Church and the kingdom of Christ—when this New Jerusalem was shown to him in vision as a city to be builded on earth according to a plan drawn in heaven, he saw "the gate of "the inner court" of that temple "that looketh toward the "east," and was told that it should be "shut the six working "days; but on the Sabbath it *shall be opened*, and in the day "of the new moon it shall be opened." (Ezek. xlvi. 1.)

I do not stay here to investigate the reason of the frequent association of new moon with Sabbath, both in the historic and prophetic Scriptures of the Old Testament, but am content to note that neither the waxing and waning moon, nor the ever-returning Sabbath, have any permanent connexion with the Mosaic dispensation.

There is not any direct mention of Sabbath-keeping during the seventy years' captivity in Babylon; and, in the silence of

Holy Scripture, it is not possible to say how the captive Israelites were wont to spend the Sabbath-day. Daniel, we know, offered prayer every day, as did David, and all devoted persons, no doubt; and his three Hebrew friends, refusing to worship other gods, put it beyond doubt that they worshipped their own God. But what difference they made on the seventh day in their administration of the affairs of the kingdom we cannot tell, nor conjecture how they obtained respite from their labours. With all their honours they were captives, and little, if at all, different from slaves in favour. The mass of their countrymen were permitted to reserve religious worship for the God whom they professed to honour, but how far they were excused from labour on the Sabbath-day is a question hard to answer.

The hundred and thirty-seventh Psalm may, on first reading, seem conclusive against the opinion that the Sabbath was kept in the Babylonish captivity, for it says that they sat down by the rivers of Babylon, hung their harps upon the willows, refused to sing the songs of Zion in a strange land, and wept when they remembered Jerusalem. The imprecations pronounced against Babylon in the same psalm show that the captives had to complain of many cruelties, and of much despite on account of their religion. Yet the circumstance of their sitting by the *rivers* and weeping suggests the idea of collective and solemn prayer on the Sabbath-day, such as it is notorious they made on that day in other countries of their dispersion in later times, and rather points to the conclusion that the Sabbath-day was not neglected but sacredly observed, at least by the more devout. It must also be remembered that their case in Babylonia was exceptional, and that solemn decrees had been repeatedly published by Nebuchadnezzar during his long reign, in honour of the God of Daniel, and of Shadrach, Meshach, and Abed-nego.

Their tenacious remembrance of Jerusalem, not only expressed by the writer of the psalm, but manifested by Daniel and his companions, by Ezekiel, Nehemiah, and others, strengthens the persuasion that they obeyed that law which required the Israelites to keep the Sabbath in their dwelling-places, and that the Hebrews were so prone to forget what it was their duty to remember, as to forbid the belief that if these could have abandoned their Sabbath they would have retained so strong, so sacred, and so endearing a remembrance of their holy city; and that when those were dead who had seen it in their youth, they would have cherished, while Sabbathless, so lively a sense of their religious faith. It is true that they had no solemn psalmody, without which a nation can hardly be expected to have much religious life or gladness. They had no ministering priesthood, no sacrifices, no festivals. Yet something they must have had to sustain their national spirit, save them from the gods of Babylon and Assyria, and preserve them in some degree of outward unity. Probably, most probably, that something was the weekly assemblages in synagogues or oratories by the river-side and other remote situations, away from heathen interruption. If this is not affirmed in the psalm, it certainly is hinted.

Again, we must bear in mind that the Sabbatic observances before the giving of the law were not, so far as we know, accompanied with ritual observances and holy convocations, and might be continued without them by prisoners of war and by wandering strangers. Until late in the age of Moses, there was no renewing of the shewbread, no changing the bands of Levites nor relieving the guards. But they had a great increase of knowledge, aided, no doubt, by the wisdom of Daniel and the counsels of Ezekiel and other holy and inspired men. We cannot believe that they were Sabbathless.

CHAPTER VI.

AFTER THE CAPTIVITY.

For the due observance of a Sabbath there must be an adaptation of society. Such an adaptation there was after the exode from Egypt, brought about by an isolation of the Israelites from all other peoples, under a system of miraculous provisions, administered with supreme and absolute authority. But such means were never employed before nor since. There was therefore no Sabbath in Egypt, and how far the sanctification of the day was carried on in Babylonia, we are not able to ascertain.

Not less than ninety years was spent in the reconstitution of society, from the time when Zerubbabel led up the first company to Jerusalem in the reign of Cyrus, to the day when first Nehemiah solemnly re-established the worship of God in the second Temple. By that time the necessary legal guards were provided, and the public mind was prepared by diligent religious teaching.

On that day "the children of Israel were assembled with " fasting, and with sackclothes, and earth upon them." The Book of Nehemiah contains an account of their separation from strangers; their confession of sins, the public reading and interpretation of the Book of the Law, and worship offered to the Lord their God. (Nehem. viii., ix.) Then followed a solemn benediction and a commemorative prayer. The commemoration began with the commencement of the Mosaic history at the creation of heaven and earth, touched on the call of Abraham, and proceeded with the great covenant, the visitation of Israel in Egypt, allusion to the events related fully in the Book of Exodus, and the giving of the Law on Sinai. "Thou camest down," said the preacher, "upon "Mount Sinai, and spakest with them from heaven, and *gavest* "them right judgments, and true laws, good statutes and "commandments: and *madest known* unto them thy holy Sab- "bath, and commandedst them precepts, statutes, and laws, "by the hand of Moses thy servant."

Here there is a careful discrimination of language in the verbs *thou gavest*, ותתן, and thou *madest known*, הודעת. Right judgments and true laws not previously in existence were then given, and the Lord's Sabbath, which men had neglected, was made known after it had been hidden, so to speak, for centuries. No less distinct in the history of their fathers was another *gift* and another *discovery*—the gift of corn and money in their sacks, and the making known of Joseph to his brethren. (Nehem. ix. 13, 14.) After the memorial-prayer, the assembled multitude made a sure covenant and wrote it, and the princes, Levites, and priests set seal to it. After covenanting to separate themselves from heathens by breaking off every unlawful alliance, they first of all engaged that if the people of the land should bring ware or any victuals on the Sabbath-day to sell, they would not buy it of them on the Sabbath or on the holy day. This being promised, they further engaged to provide maintenance for the worship of God and for his ministers, but to the Sabbath, above all, they gave pre-eminence, as had before been given. (Nehem. x. 31—39.)

There was not much difficulty made, at first, in carrying on the Temple services, nor was there any complaint that the great festivals were not kept, or that the strictly prescribed oblations and sacrifices were not presented. The recovery of some of the ancient grandeur was pleasant. To have a city, a temple, and a name, was worth some trouble and even some cost. To eclipse the pride of the Samaritans was no small consideration. But it was not agreeable to those new citizens to give up certain petty gains on God's own day, and nothing less than stern authority could bring them to it. The clear account of Nehemiah has been so often quoted, that repetition here might seem superfluous, yet it must be repeated, and that in the very words of the narrator.

"In those days I saw in Judah some treading wine-presses
" on the Sabbath, and bringing in sheaves, and lading asses;
" as also wine, grapes, and figs, and all manner of burdens,
" which they brought into Jerusalem on the Sabbath-day:
" and I testified against them in the day wherein they sold
" victuals. There dwelt men of Tyre also therein which
" brought fish, and all manner of ware, and sold on the Sab-
" bath unto the children of Judah, and in Jerusalem. Then
" I contended with the nobles of Judah, and said unto them,
" What evil thing is this that ye do, and profane the Sabbath-
" day? Did not your fathers thus, and did not our God
" bring all this evil upon us, and upon this city? Yet ye
" bring more wrath upon Israel by profaning the Sabbath.
" And it came to pass, that when the gates of Jerusalem
" began to be dark before the Sabbath, I commanded that
" the gates should be shut, and charged that they should not
" be opened till after the Sabbath: and some of my servants
" set I at the gates, that there should no burden be brought
" in on the Sabbath-day. So the merchants and sellers of
" all kind of ware lodged without Jerusalem once or twice.
" Then I testified against them, and said unto them, Why
" lodge ye about the wall? If ye do so again, I will lay
" hands on you. From that time forth came they no more
" on the Sabbath. And I commanded the Levites that they
" should cleanse themselves, and that they should come and
" keep the gates, to sanctify the Sabbath-day." (Nehem. xiii. 15—22.)

The reflection of a moment must convince any thoughtful person that if the Sabbath had not been kept in Jerusalem little good would have been done. Neither priests nor Levites would have been at their posts. The altars would have been forsaken, the courts of God's house deserted, and confused crowds of Jews and Gentiles would have filled Jerusalem with the uproar of traffic the most unhallowed on the sacred day. But when trade was entirely suspended, and the Tyrian fisherman and merchant, no less than the Judean husbandman and city chapman, were compelled to cease from business—when servant, and slave, and foreigner were all to lay aside their burdens and cease their noise—then the songs of Zion could swell full-voiced with solemn sound, and, in the repose of the earthly city during those consecrated hours, the inhabitants would conceive a longing for the heavenly rest.

But the godless could not enjoy that which had no charm for the mind not educated to its enjoyment. Heathen visitors, whose very religion consisted in obscene rites and bacchanalian revelry, would pass the day wearily. Others would be deeply impressed with admiration, contrasting the day of rest and piety in the chief city of Judah, and thenceforth in all the cities of the land, with the days of sacrificial slaughter and profligacy in their own cities, when the Phœnicians, for example, were abandoned to the debauchery of Ashtaroth, or the Canaanites were pouring out the blood of innocents at the altars of Moloch, their insatiate king. If the successors of Nehemiah and his servants had been equally faithful with himself and them, the Sabbath of restored Jerusalem would have distinguished that land from all the world beside, and would have extorted from the greatest of nations admiration of those very Jews whom they scowled upon as contemptible barbarians.

The happy state of things established under the government of Nehemiah did not continue long, but for so long as it did last the effects were very salutary. Nevertheless, his nation could not yet be restored. Prophecy was departing. Sacrifice itself became poor and intermittent. It was reserved for Christianity to do for the world what the Law of Moses was not intended to effect, and what Judaism never could pretend to do. The world was now in one of its crises of transition, and the Jews, brought into intercourse with Persians and then with Greeks, began to interchange ideas. The writings of the great Prophets anterior to the captivity, and those of Ezekiel and Daniel, with two or three of later date, being now read and studied with increasing reverence, cast new light upon the Jewish mind—for this remnant of Israelites now takes the name of Judah—and this is the "old time" of which the Apostle speaks when he says that Moses and the Prophets were read in the synagogues every Sabbath-day, and the reading brought clearer light and prepared both Jews and Gentiles for profounder studies.

Never was the value of the Sabbath made more manifest, for now those persons who feared God met together on that day to make mention of his name, and this they did habitually, as we learn from the Prophet Malachi. Perhaps it was then, when the Sabbath became so solemnly acknowledged, and so manifestly the chief part of the Jews' religion, that Gentiles could only think of it as a Jewish institution; and so uninstructed persons to this day regard it. But certainly it was far more effectual for the preservation of revealed truth than all the magnificent ceremonial of Solomon and Herod, more even than the departing ritual of Moses.

Next come the times of Antiochus Epiphanes and the Maccabees. Antiochus, having thought himself insulted by the people of Jerusalem, who were in too great haste to betray some satisfaction on hearing news of his death, which happened to be false, vainly determined to crush the Jews and their religion. His persecution was one of the fiercest on record, and may be classed with the Alpine dragonnades and the massacre of St. Bartholomew's day, while some of its incidents remind us of the war of the Duke of Alva in the Netherlands. His first great outrage was committed in Jerusalem, where he pillaged the Temple and carried away or destroyed its most precious objects. Having taken most of the gold he waited two years, and then sent one Apollonius, a collector of taxes, to extort as much more as possible. This man found the inhabitants of Jerusalem very much better, as we may believe, for what they had suffered. The synagogues were well frequented, as was the Temple, and Apollonius spared no pains to intimidate or bribe the people to apostasy. Many gave way, offered sacrifice to idols, and broke the Sabbath. Idolatry and Sabbath-breaking were the two signs of submission given by hundreds of Jews who so purchased favour or avoided death. (1 Macc. i. 45—54.)

It was during this war that about a thousand Jews, with their wives, children, and cattle, having fled to the mountains, hoping to rally their forces there, and make a stand against the enemy, were on one Sabbath-day attacked in caverns and slaughtered without resistance. They preferred to die rather than break God's law, as they thought they should do if they fought on that day. Thus they fell, and are worthily counted with the martyrs; but the event led their surviving brethren to consider whether the law really forbade resistance when attacked, and so delivered them helpless to their murderers. Their decision was that such is not the meaning of the commandment. They agreed that war, if it be defensive only, is not work or business in the proper meaning of the word, but a necessary self-defence, and that a Jew might lawfully fight for his life on any day. This decision has been held valid ever since, and those noble confessors, after such proofs of sincere devotion as they had given, and still gave, preferring any suffering, and even death itself, to the least appearance of apostasy, rallied all their forces, turned bravely upon the ferocious persecutors, and after a succession of victories, saw the last of them. (1 Macc. ii. 29—41.) From this time the Jews have excelled all others in their strict observance of the Sabbath, although that strictness has been sometimes perverted by self-righteousness and superstition.

Pompey, when he attacked Jerusalem, about 63 years before Christ, found the decision of Mattathias still in force. They left their enemy without any apprehension of hostile action on their part, so long as he lay inactive on the sacred day, but watched him narrowly, and if he proceeded to attack they were quite ready to accept battle.

Thus far we trace this most ancient institution free from rabbinical corruptions. These began after the Maccabean victories, but much earlier than Pompey, and after his day they multiplied with great rapidity. I therefore proceed to notice the Jewish triflings, which have much obscured its real character.

CHAPTER VII.

THE JEWISH SABBATH, OR SABBATH SPOILED WITH TRADITIONAL OBSERVANCES.

I know of no better source of information concerning the Jewish Sabbath properly so called, than the title *Shabbat* in the *Mishnah*, which contains the traditions that come to view in the New Testament. It is true that the *Mishnah* was not brought into its present form until about the year of our Lord 150; but we know that the materials are very ancient, some of them being traditions attributed to wise men who lived long before the time of Christ. A knowledge of those traditions, as found in the Mishnah, is necessary to an understanding of much that is written in the Gospels. Our present object is to ascertain the characteristics of the Jewish or Rabbinical Sabbath, just as our Lord found it.

The compiler of the title "Sabbath" begins by discoursing of two men standing in a doorway, a poor man outside and the master of the house within. The poor man reaches towards the other and gives something into his hand, or he reaches and takes something from him, and brings it away. "The poor man is guilty, and the master of the house is free." Or the master of the house is first to extend his hand, either to give or to receive; and, if to receive, also to put what he has taken into its place within. In this case he is guilty, and the poor man free. Or if their movements are simultaneous and concurrent, they are both free.

No man is to sit before a barber as the Sabbath-eve approaches, if there be not time for the barber to finish shaving him before the time of evening sacrifice begins. Neither must he commence a meal nor proceed to judge.

When the sun begins to darken, a tailor must not walk out with his needle, lest sunset should overtake him carrying it. Nor may a scribe walk out with his reed, lest he forget, and go on with it in his hand. After the Sabbath lamp is lighted one must not begin to pick the vermin from his garments, nor yet begin to read by its light, for this would be counted servile work. This was determined in a celebrated conference between some Hillelites and Shammaites, in the chamber of Khananiah, son of Goron, where eighteen hard questions were settled under his presidency.

The schools of Hillel and Shammai both agree that goods ought not to be sold to a Gentile so near the Sabbath hour that he or his beast should have to carry it away when the hour comes; and cautions of the same kind are multiplied.

We find some exact injunctions concerning the kind of fuel that may be used for Sabbath fires, and the oil proper to be burnt in Sabbath lamps. The lamp, it is noted, must not be extinguished in the night, if the motive be to save the oil; but it may be put out if the motive be to avoid keeping a sick person awake by its light. Unlawful management of lamps on the Sabbath is a sin, as they said, for which women are punished with death in childbed.

A man must say three things in his house on the eve of the Sabbath: *Hast thou paid the tithes? Have you prepared the food? Then light the lamp.* If there be doubt whether it be light or dark, then it is too late for any of these things to be done.

All culinary affairs are to be regulated by scrupulously minute directions, which it must have been extremely difficult to follow without numberless failures and endless disputes.

"With what," they ask, "may a beast be permitted to

"walk out of the stable?" The answer is, that a camel may walk out with his muzzle; a she-camel with her nose-ring; a Lydian ass with his bit; a horse with his chain; all beasts with what they have to hold them. And if they need washing they may go into the water and wash themselves. The ass may carry his own saddle. Rams may go leashed together. Ewes, having their teats bound up that the milk may dry away, may in like manner walk out as they are. Rabbi Judah makes a very fine distinction as to goats—he permits them to go about with their udders bound up for drying away the milk, but not if it is to preserve milk for the dairy.

Camels are placed under some special restraints, and so are asses. An ass must not walk forth with its saddle, unless the saddle be made fast on it. The animal must not carry a bell, even though the bell be muffled, nor may it have a yoke on its neck, nor a thong on its foot. A cock must not go abroad with a thread on its leg, nor a ram drawing the cart under its tail,* nor a sheep having grass in its mouth. The heifer may not carry her yoke, nor the cow her porcupine upon her udder,† nor a cord about her horns. Rabbi Eliezer, son of Azariah, allowed his cow to carry a cord on the Sabbath, to the great scandal of the wise men.

"But how may a woman go abroad, and how may she "not?" The answer is that she may not go with a dashy head-dress—and some varieties of head-dresses are specified. She must not wear trinkets unless they are so attached as to make part of her garments. Concerning jewels and perfumes, the wise men have never been quite unanimous, but all of them are strict in various degrees.

---

* Sheep having large fatty tails, which are often saved from dragging in the mire by a sort of little cart attached, which the animal draws as it goes, literally carrying its tail behind it.

† A prickly skin to prevent the calf from sucking.

A man may not walk out with sword, nor bow, nor shield, nor sling, nor spear. Rabbi Eliezer did indeed allow him to go on the Sabbath so equipped, saying that weapons were but part of a soldier. Other wise men, on the contrary, said that weapons were a soldier's disgrace, forasmuch as it is written that they shall beat their swords into ploughshares, and their spears into pruning-hooks. But they allow a man to wear spurs on the Sabbath.

And how may a lame man go on the Sabbath? He may go on his crutch, if it be not padded for the sake of comfort.

A person might carry a locust's egg or a fox's tooth, if he carried it as a charm, or a clove, if he had it as a medicine, or at least he had permission to carry such trifles to charm away his pains, according to the indulgent sentence of Rabbi Meir; but other wise men forbade them utterly.*

From these examples it may be seen how the Pharisees trifled; not perhaps at first, for in some of these rules it is possible to discern a good reason under the guise of a precept almost if not quite ridiculous; but the process of trifling went on with inevitable rapidity from lower to lower. Other examples will be derived from the same source when we come to consider certain passages in the Gospels which will be presented for illustration.

I have not observed any indication of such rabbinic trifling in the times of the Old Testament. Rabbinism, as I have endeavoured to show elsewhere,† was not begun in the days of Nehemiah, when the observance of the Sabbath was revived once more. Nothing of the kind appears in the book of Malachi. The Maccabean history is also clear of every vestige of this kind of superstition, for which the times

---

* Mishnah, Order of Feasts, Title Sabbath, chapters i.—vi.

† History of the Karaite Jews, chapters ii., iii., iv.

were far too grave. People died martyrs for eternal verities, and were of a spirit far too noble and earnest to brook such childish trifling. It is therefore at variance with historic evidence to attribute follies like these of the days following Hillel to the age of Moses, or to any other age much before the birth of Christ. After that time traditionist principles were in active operation, but the chapters of the Mishnah, as they come to us, were not yet compiled, as there is abundant evidence to prove. It is, I must repeat, an abuse of language to call that Sabbath Jewish which was alike acknowledged by Prophets and Apostles. The Jewish Sabbath is what I have now been endeavouring to exemplify, not in my own language, but simply as I find it set forth by the pen of Rabbi Judah the Holy, about the year of our Lord 150, in a collection of sentences all, or nearly all, of date considerably older.

But although these are characteristics of the Jewish Sabbath, properly so called, it would be untrue to say that the Jews had no higher views of that blessed institution than can be gathered from the Mishnah. The Jews were not all Pharisees nor all Traditionists, nor have they ever been. The history of Karaism affords abundant proof that in every age since the close of the Old Testament canon and the officious labours of the Sanhedrim, there has been a strong party of honest believers in Divine revelation, living in avowed opposition to the traditionism of the Pharisees and the scepticism of the Sadducees. It is more than probable that multitudes of thoughtful and conscientious Jews, between the times of the heroically-faithful Maccabees and the ministry of our Lord Jesus Christ, had a more distinct perception of the leading truths of inspired Scripture, and a better sense of the obligation of God's holy laws, with little care for the comfortless trifling of their less enlightened brethren.

Philo, the eminent Alexandrian Jew, may be accepted as a faithful witness. Philo lived in the time of our Lord and his Apostles. He was a man of high rank, a thorough Jew, extensively acquainted with the affairs of his nation, and its chosen advocate to the Roman Emperor in one critical conjuncture, if not more. In his time the Second Temple was standing, fresh in the architectural grandeur given it by Herod, and the worship was conducted without any restriction with all the pomp which the Jews were able and willing to command. Philo, not less than other Egyptian Jews, would go to Jerusalem at the great festivals, and observe the religious life of their Palestinian brethren at all times of the year. He also saw them in several other countries, and corresponded with them over yet a wider circle. His account of the Sabbath is therefore of great historic value, and no statement of a later writer, much less of any in these times of our own, could compare with it in authority.

Unlike some of our contemporaries, he is mindful to call the sacred seventh day *the birthday of the world*. He says that Moses assigned to the *Hexade* (six days) the birth of the several portions of the world; but the *Hebdomade* (seven days) a period independent and uncompounded with any other in the whole round of seasons, sheds its light upon the lesser term. All that the six days produced, the seventh day showed to be now made complete in full perfection. Therefore we duly hail it as birthday of the world.*

Speaking of God, Creator of the Universe, not only of a part thereof, he describes him as surveying the whole aggregate of creatures, and using each one in its turn for his own glory. Then he relates how, when the heavens gave no rain, as in Egypt, He made the earth yield water to irrigate its own

---

* "De Septenario," sect. 6.

surface, as it does by the overflowing of the Nile; and so in the Arabian wilds, where the earth yields no food, God the Creator caused the air to send down manna with the dew, and gave honour to the seventh day by raining double on the sixth day for the supply of his people while they rested.*

He does not trace the institution of the Sabbath to Moses, but to the time of the Creation. He derives his knowledge from the same fountain as we, and describes the manner in which the Jews of his time pass the day. They learn what he calls the *philosophy* of their fathers, doubtless using the word as equivalent with the Hebrew *wisdom*, which, in the common language of the Old Testament and the rabbinical books, means *religion*, or religious knowledge. They devote the time, he says, to the understanding and contemplation of the things of nature—whether as the secularist now professes to do, or studying natural objects as did Solomon and David his father, and as Philo himself did, when he spoke of the irrigation of Egypt by the Nile, and the descent of manna with the dew in Arabia—in what sense he means I cannot say, but certainly should think the latter. But the remainder of the passage now quoted is more distinct. "For the places for "prayer, προσευκτήρια, which are in the cities, what are they "but places where they learn prudence, and manliness, and "sobriety, and justice, piety towards God, and holiness, and "every kind of virtue, what are they else but schools for the "learning and exercise of things heavenly and divine?"†
"In their Sabbath assemblies, which are numerously attended, "they appear decently attired, take their seats with decorum, "and listen attentively. The multitude hear in silence while "the Law is read, and the silence is only broken by any

---

* "De Vitâ Moysis," lib. i., sect. 36.
† "De Vitâ Moysis," lib. iii., sect. 27.

"questions which may haply be suggested. Some one of the priests presides. One of the ancient men reads the sacred laws, and either he or some one of his venerable brethren expounds the meaning."*

Josephus does not write with the fulness and earnestness of Philo, but is in perfect agreement with him when he says that the Jews "set apart the seventh day for learning their customs and laws, which they think it right to understand and reflect upon, as they reflect on anything else, that they may avoid sin."†

So do these witnesses give their evidence, one of them rather in the style of a Karaite than of a common Jew. If we were not aware of the state of religion at that time, when the masters of the text and the teachers of tradition were in sharp conflict, we might fall into the mistake of supposing that while the sages who collected materials for the Mishnah were thus promoting an interior discipline among the Jews themselves, Philo and Josephus were giving themselves to the establishment of an exoteric method, and presenting Judaism to the Gentiles under a reasonable aspect just as they wished them to regard it. The suspicion does sometimes return to our mind, but it cannot be confidently entertained. The truth seems to be that, if we would see Judaism as it was in the time of our Lord, we must hear it described by the historian, philosopher, and apologist on one side, by the teacher of tradition on the other, and after all have recourse to the New Testament for a complete account of all.

We know how cordially Roman satirists despised Jewish Sabbatarians, and with what contemptuous ignorance some of them were used to mock their scruples; but we cannot

---

* "Phil. Jud. Fragm. ex Euseb. Præp. Evang.," viii. 7.
† "Joseph. Antiq.," xvi. li. 4.

fail to perceive that the Sabbath, however deteriorated, was a sign between God and his people whereby they were effectually distinguished from the heathen world. Here again Philo bears witness. Every nation, he says, has its own laws and customs. The Athenians have theirs, the Spartans theirs, and they will not borrow from another. The Egyptians and Syrians hate each others' manners. The inhabitants of Europe and those of Asia cherish their mutual antipathies. But although the Jews differ from them all, and in no respect more than in their observance of the Sabbath, this peculiarity does not provoke any such repugnance.

" Barbarians, Greeks, inhabitants alike of continents and
" islands, nations of the East and West, Europe, Asia, all
" the world from one extremity to the other, look on it with
" admiration. Who does not thoroughly honour that holy
" seventh day? They admire its rest from labour, and the
" refreshment it affords to all who live under its influence, to
" freemen and to slaves; and not to men only, but even to
" the beasts of burden. The very herds of cattle on this
" day range at large, and seem to render free service to the
" Lord of nature. The very trees of the forest are exempt
" from all demands, for on this day not a leaf is plucked nor
" a twig broken. The crops and harvests, although ripe,
" stand in the fields untouched, and are free from depreda-
" tion." *

Such was the case, no doubt, wherever the Jew had lands which he could call his own, and even where he was an alien; yet, where he could gather a few brethren around him, and form a little settlement, it is notable that such communities have been always respected—at least until a corrupted Chris-

---

* " De Vitâ Moysis," ii. 4.

tianity has raised its crusade against them. In Spain, for example, they blessed the fruits of the earth on the lands of Gentiles, even of Christians; and, in the Council of Elliberis, the Christian bishops forbade their flocks to accept the Jewish blessings, lest the clerical benedictions should be thereby nullified.

The Tyrian merchants, as we learn from the Carthaginian history, and as we read in the latest Carthaginian inscriptions, carried with them the worship of the old Canaanitish gods; but the Hebrew emigrants did not so carry into the lands of their captivity the idolatry adopted by their brethren at home.

CHAPTER VIII.

THE JEWISH SABBATH DURING OUR LORD'S MINISTRY.

The synagogue services were obviously calculated to prepare the public mind for the more perfect services which are found essential to the maintenance of Christianity. A synagogue—where perhaps one or two families met together, and became the beginning of a congregation that was never very numerous—was literally a *meeting-house*, בית כנסה, in the very simple style of Hebrew nomenclature. It is said that about this time there were no fewer than four hundred such meeting-houses in Jerusalem. Allowing for some exaggeration, there can be no doubt that there were many, and that they abounded in other towns. In those congregations our Lord Jesus Christ pronounced some discourses and performed some miracles, but he often appeared only as an Israelite worshipper among his fellows, even after he " began to be thirty years of age." Before that time he did not officiate at all. But, during the years of his public ministry, he most fully gave Divine sanction to the sanctification of the Sabbath by the ministration of the Word of God and prayer. In his memorable conversation with the Samaritan woman he intimated in the clearest language that spiritual worship would be offered up to God, in like manner, in all parts of the world. Far more emphatically he foretold to his disciples the destruction of the Temple, and on another occasion he spoke to them of the continuance of synagogues, and the power exerted by those congregations as corporate authorities.

Very soon after his baptism and temptation, "He came " to Nazareth, where he had been brought up : and, as his

" custom was, he went into the synagogue on the Sabbath-day,
" and stood up for to read." Then was " delivered unto him
" the book," or roll, " of the Prophet Esaias. And when he
" had *unrolled*, ἀναπτύξας, the book, he found the place
" where it was written, the Spirit of the Lord is upon me,"
&c. "And he closed the book, and he gave it again to the
" minister, and sat down. And the eyes of all them that
" were in the synagogue were fastened on him. And he
" began to say unto them," &c. (Luke iv. 16—21.)

This first account of a synagogue visit in the Gospel narrative is now quoted for the sake of its circumstantial description, which enables us to identify one of the synagogue customs of that time with a form prescribed in the Mishnah as obligatory, on a different occasion indeed, but observed when the Law or the Prophets was read, in order to maintain the proper decorum, and to show becoming reverence to the sacred books. If the very words of the following regulation had been then incorporated in a written law, universally recognized, the Lord could not have complied more exactly with its requirement. "The *Khazzan* of the synagogue
" takes the book of the Law, and gives it to the *Chief* of
" the synagogue. The Chief of the synagogue gives it to
" the *Ságan*,* and the Ságan gives it to the *Chief Priest.*
" The Chief Priest stands up, having received it, and reads
" it standing." "Then he rolls up the volume of the Law,

---

* This is originally a Chaldee word, סגן, the name given to the *Vicar* of the Chief Priest. The Chief of the synagogue receives the roll from his *Khazzan*, or minister who has charge of it for him, and delivers it to the Chief Priest for *his* use as administrator of the Law. The Ságan assists the Priest. In the synagogue at Nazareth there was no administration of discipline, nor was our Lord a priest; but as an Israelite his relation was with the synagogue only for worship and instruction.

"and lays (what he has read) in his bosom, and says, 'More than what I have read to you is written in this book.'"*

No man might sit, nor even lean, while reading from the sacred book. It is said that Rabbi Samuel, son of Isaac, once came into a synagogue while some one was interpreting as he read, leaning at ease against a pillar. Offended at the sight, the Rabbi approached the careless reader, and bade him cease. "This cannot be permitted," said he, "for as the Law was delivered with solemnity, it must be read by us with reverence."† The Prophet of Nazareth stood up while He read, and did not sit down until He had closed the book, and delivered it to the minister. He did not read much. It was a general rule that the reader should not deliver less than twenty-one lines from a Prophet, yet on the Sabbath-day, if there was an interpretation or sermon, he might read even so little as three, but not less.‡

The profound silence of the Nazarean congregation during the interpretation which followed after the brief reading from Isaiah lxi. exactly corresponds with the silent attention described by Philo in a passage quoted above, and the outburst of noise which followed does not in the least disagree with the remainder of that description.

When the Saviour taught thus on the Sabbath, He gave an authoritative example to his servants. (Luke iv. 31.) The Prophet of God led the way for ministers in all ages, teaching them how to teach. Their duty is to *teach* the people. They are not to entertain them with popular lectures, nor to attract crowds by rhetorical artifice. Instruction, exhortation, and prayer take the place of material sacrifices, which He has set aside by the offering of himself. Observe well that, from the

---

* NASHIM. Sota, vii. 7. † Megilloth, xxi.
‡ Soferim, xii.

day when his mother brought the humble offering on occasion of her purification after his birth, we read no more of any Levitical offering presented in connexion with himself. He came to set aside that priesthood, and held no such communication with its members as might have been otherwise expected. But no one observed the Sabbath more strictly than He, and had He meant to set that institution aside with the Mosaic dispensation, it is not likely that He would have chosen the Sabbath-day for his public teaching, for there were other days which He might have taken also for those visits to the synagogues. There were *three* synagogue-days in the week, the second, the fourth, and the seventh. He marked the seventh strictly, and seems to have passed by the other two without any special note. As for the synagogues, if he had not intended to make any further use of those places of sacred assemblage, we cannot conceive it likely that He would have sanctified them by his constant and reverential presence.

As He " adorned and beautified the holy estate of matrimony " with his presence and first miracle that He wrought in Cana of " Galilee," so did he adorn the ministration of saving truth with many miracles in those Sabbath congregations. So, for example, in the synagogue of Capernaum, where the people were astonished at his doctrine, and contrasted the authority manifest in his delivery with the hesitancy and servile indecision of the scribes when He cast the spirit of an unclean devil out of a man. (Luke iv. 33.) So in another synagogue while he was teaching, he released a woman from an infirmity which had oppressed and bound her eighteen years. There she was, her body bowed down with weakness, and her soul prostrate with despair; but Jesus laid his hands on her, saying, " Woman, thou art loosed from thine infirmity, and imme-" diately she was made straight, and glorified God." (Luke xiii. 13.)

Again, in another synagogue, also on the Sabbath-day, did He adorn the day, and show that it should be consecrated with deeds of mercy, saying to a man, even unsolicited, "Stretch "forth thine hand; and he stretched it forth, and it was re-"stored whole as the other." (Matt. xii. 13.)

Now, let those who would maintain that this is but a Jewish institution, relaxed or even set aside by the Founder of a superior system, spare themselves time to study his words and actions a little more closely before they arrive at so unreasonable a conclusion. We will examine the one authentic record, and judge for ourselves. How did He teach?

"At that time Jesus went on the Sabbath-day through the "corn; and his disciples were an hungred, and began to "pluck the ears of corn, and to eat. But when the Pharisees "saw it, they said unto him, Behold, thy disciples do that "which is not lawful to do upon the Sabbath-day. But He "said unto them, Have ye not read what David did when he "was an hungred, and they that were with him; how he "entered into the house of God, and did eat the shewbread, "which was not lawful for him to eat, neither for them which "were with him, but only for the priests? Or have ye not "read in the Law, how that on the Sabbath-days the priests "in the temple profane the Sabbath, and are blameless? But "I say unto you, that in this place is one greater than the "temple. But if ye had known what this meaneth, I will "have mercy, and not sacrifice, ye would not have condemned "the guiltless. For the Son of Man is Lord even of the "Sabbath-day." (Matt. xii. 1—8.)

In accusing our Lord of doing what it was not lawful to do, they touched the cardinal point whereon the whole question turns. At the Creation it was ordained that the day should be *sanctified*. When the Law was given on Mount Sinai, it was ordained that all ordinary business should cease; and that there might not be either necessity or excuse for carrying it on, the people were commanded to do all that they had to do within the six working days. In the provisions for Temple-worship every necessary arrangement was made for due observance of the Sabbath, and not only for its due observance in conjunction with the great festivals, but for its independent observance, with such foresight that, in the course of ages, when the Temple-worship should be extinct, and the priesthood abolished, the fourth commandment of the Decalogue should remain in full force, and the sanctity of the Sabbatic institution abide intact. In pursuance of this design, the document in which it is described not only remained entire and distinct, but received the most explicit sanction of him who came to fulfil the Law, and also to establish that system of mercy which even the Law was given to prepare the way for. Nothing could be more explicit than his recognition of this very Decalogue when He quoted it literally to one who came to him inquiring what he should do to inherit eternal life. (Mark x. 19.)

Thus did the foundation of the Sabbath remain unshaken, but the Pharisees, who claimed its privileges for themselves and their nation only, had adopted another and very different foundation. This was the fundamental principle then orally maintained, and soon afterwards incorporated with the Mishnah. They call it in that compilation *the root of the Sabbath*, עיקר שבת. This root, however, is but negative, and the full notion of sanctifying it does not satisfy. It includes not any sanctification of the day to God, but only treats in minute particulars of actions forbidden or allowed. This is the weak foundation which our Lord rejects, but He carefully maintains the other, which we see to be alike consistent with every moral principle of the Old Testament and the New.

The rabbis explained their fundamental principle by laying down a scale of primary and secondary works, calling the former אבות מלאכות, *fathers of works.*, "The primary works "are forty save one. Sowing, Ploughing, Reaping, Gathering in Bundles, Thrashing, Winnowing, Cleansing, Grinding, Sifting, Roasting, Boiling, Shearing the Wool, Washing the Wool, Carding it, Dyeing it, Spinning, Weaving, Knotting two threads, Twisting two threads, Breaking two threads, Binding, Unbinding, Sewing two stitches, Ripping to Sew up again, Hunting a Kid, Killing it, Skinning it, Salting it, Dressing the Skin, Scraping it, Cutting it, Writing two letters, Blotting out in order to write two letters, Building, Pulling down, Quenching, Kindling, Beating with a hammer, Removing from place to place. Behold, these are the primary works, forty save one."*

Now this is not an enumeration of all varieties of industrial occupation. It falls immeasurably short of the letter of the commandment, and could only serve to minister endless occasion of debate by its omissions, if narrowly interpreted, or by its inevitable uncertainty, and by the frequent difficulty in ascertaining what is a *secondary work*, תולדה, and under which of the primary works many insignificant operations might be rightly classed. After all the laborious trifling of casuists men walked in their own ways, spoke their own words, and did their own pleasure, saving the thirty-nine categories of primary works, if they were clever enough to do it, or if their wise men were ingenious enough to invent reasons for dispensation.

On the other hand, almost any conceivable action might be included under one or other of them, as in the case of our Lord's disciples in the corn-field, when the Pharisees, no

---

* MOED, Shabbat, vii. 1, 2.

doubt, condemned the plucking an ear of corn as a kind of reaping, and the rubbing a grain of corn between the fingers as a kind of thrashing, which would be a double breach of oral law, a twice-doing that which it was not lawful to do. If such interpretations were to be allowed, any law might be made ridiculous, as, indeed, the Pharisees made God's law seem to be. "Hunting," they would say, " is a kind of " primary work. To chase a flea and crack it is as much a " kind of hunting and a kind of slaughtering as if the flea " were a camel. Therefore, on the Sabbath, you must not " catch fleas."

The word *law* has different meanings as it is used by different persons. With the Pharisee it is the law of Moses not as it is written, but as the wise men of his own school, or a majority of them, agree to understand it, or to have it understood. With our Lord it is the law of Moses plainly written, as any honest and intelligent reader understands it. He, therefore, was not used to make a traditional sentence the subject of debate, for thereby He would allow such a sentence a certain character of authority, and, by even seeming to suspend his judgment for an instant on the chance of its validity, would seem to recognize the right of a traditionist to be heard in competition with the inspired lawgiver. *That* He never would allow, but entered at once upon the subject of inquiry as it is treated in Holy Scripture, or may be judged of thence. In the present case He refers the Pharisees to a precedent recorded in the First Book of Samuel (xxi. 1—6), where we read what David did when he was hungry, and they that were with him; how he entered into the house of God and ate the shewbread, which it was not lawful for him or them to eat, but only the priests. On referring to the passage we find that David did not lay hands on the table of shewbread, regardless of the law, when under the pressure of hunger, but that, hungry as he was, he went into the Tabernacle and asked the priest for such bread as he had, and that Ahimelech, not having any other than the hallowed bread, offered him that, and he accepted it. The hot bread, we see, was put upon the table—which shows that the emergency occurred on the Sabbath-day—and David and his men, instead of the priests, ate the loaves which were then taken off. The humane action of the chief priest was justified by a pressing necessity, and the Talmudists themselves allow that *the urgency of saving life*, פקוח נפש, drives away the Sabbath.

That instance shut the mouths of the Pharisees; but it does much more. It teaches us, what it should have taught them, the meaning of a Divine—not a traditional—sentence, that God will have mercy, and not sacrifice. It confirms that for which we contend, that the Sabbath-law, as it is laid down in the Old Testament, and expounded in the New, is consistent with the highest humanity and mercy.

And this is confirmed by the saying of our Lord on this occasion, recorded by St. Mark: "The Sabbath was made "for man, and not man for the Sabbath." (Mark ii. 27.) Not that man may deal with the Sabbath as he pleases, to set it aside at pleasure, or to use it for convenience, as he may choose; for Christ, not man, is Lord of this graciously-appointed institution.

The allusion to the priests in the Temple requires explanation. The phrase "profane the Sabbath" is not unusual. It occurs, for example, in the Mishnah, where it is said that "on two months *they profane the Sabbath*—in Nisan and in "Tishri—for in these months the messengers go forth (on "the Sabbath, if necessary) into Syria, and in them they ap- "point (the time) of the feasts; and while the Temple was "standing *they profaned the Sabbath* in all the months, for the "sake of making ready the offering."* Maimonides explains this to mean the additional offering which the law appointed to be made on each of the New Moons. The first day of the month often falls on the first day of the week with us, whose calendar months are solar, and yet oftener with the Jews, whose months were lunar. Whenever that coincidence took place, it was said that they profaned the Sabbath by those active labours which were necessary for making ready the offering for the feast when they would otherwise be resting for the Sabbath. But that profaning was far indeed from being sinful. It was not a common business, but the Lord's business, which they did, and thereby rendered obedience to his command. Peril of death, then, and the pressure of a separate Divine obligation, justified and even required a temporary departure from the letter of one law in particular, and ensured a due regard for the spirit of it.

The same authority says that "they deliver a woman on "the Sabbath, and bring the midwife to her from one place "to another, and *profane the Sabbath* for her that they may "bind the (infant's) navel." †

To save life or to preserve it, or to fulfil a Divine obligation, warranted what is called conventionally a profaning of the Sabbath; and in our Lord's declaration that He is Lord of the Sabbath-day, He unequivocally assumes a Divine right to do whatever seems good to himself on that day. But at the same time he asserts that Sabbath-observance is not a part of the Mosaic dispensation. The Son of Man, as we may all know, was never called Lord of the Passover, or of Purim. He who is the same yesterday, to-day, and for ever, is not Lord of things transient, but of things abiding, such as is the day of holy rest, a day that will return faithful as the

---

* Rosh Hashannah, i. 4. † Shabbath, xviii. 3.

sun in the firmament, as long as time endures. Therefore, it is not Jewish.

While, however, we Christians look up for guidance to our Divine Master, as being Lord of the Sabbath, we remember that He is also *our* Lord, and seek to ascertain what is *his* estimate of things called Jewish before we venture to determine what shall be ours. In relation to the Sabbath there are certain additions to the Law of the Old Testament which are noted in the New without a word of either censure or approval. Yet, in the lips of Christ or his inspired servant, mention without censure may almost be taken for approval, and here are two examples.

First, the *Preparation*, or παράσκευη. So they called the day before the Sabbath, because the last three hours of that day were spent in preparing food to be eaten on the Sabbath, and in getting everything ready for Sabbath use. The Rabbis taught that the gathering double measure of manna on the sixth day was the precedent to be followed, but the manna was gathered early in the morning, not between three o'clock and sunset. The Karaites, on the other hand, have declared openly against this " preparation," saying truly enough that there is no command in the Bible for an addition of three hours of common time to the sacred time, which cannot be either prolonged or shortened.* Yet all the four Evangelists mention the Preparation † with allowance, to say the least, perhaps rather with approval. This mention occurs in their narratives of the Crucifixion, and so occurs as to remind us that the institution of those preparation-customs was ancient—so ancient that the sixth day of the week was no

---

* Rule's History of the Karaite Jews. Longmans. 1870. P. 15, *seq.*

† Matt. xxvii. 62, Mark xv. 42, Luke xxiii. 54, John xix. 14, 31, 42.

longer counted in order with the rest, but called "The Pre-"paration." The custom, we presume, was considerably more ancient than the name.

Second, the Sabbath-day's journey is determined by *the Bound of the Sabbath*. This is the limit found by measuring outwards from the wall of a city a distance that is variously estimated, some saying that it is *one* mile, and others *two*. The question of measurement is discussed in the Talmud,* but for our present purpose it is not material which way the decision turns. The Sabbath-day's journey is mentioned in the Acts of the Apostles, with relation to Bethany, the scene of our Lord's Ascension. Our Lord, himself, it would seem, alluded to it in an exhortation to his disciples that they should pray that their flight might not be in the winter, nor on the Sabbath-day.† For how could they escape the Roman army outside Jerusalem if they were kept back by the Sabbath-law as then accepted, within a radius of one mile or even two miles from the city? Yet the restraint on Sabbath excursion might be very salutary; and although it could not be enforced by the letter of the Mosaic law, it was quite consistent with the spirit. As the Evangelists pass these two observances without disapproval, we may safely do the same. The spirit of such additions is not Rabbinical, for the Rabbis rather sought to evade the strictness of God's law than to increase it.

Before dismissing this part of our survey we step into the outer world, and glance at the true Jewish Sabbath from a pagan point of view, ascertaining the impression it made on the mind of the Gentiles. From their view the domestic life and the religious observances of the worshippers of the true God were for the most part concealed; but the absence of

---

* Eirubin, v. 8 9.   † Acts i. 12.

the Jew from his accustomed place of business one day of every seven drew towards him general attention, and some of their sayings tell their misapprehension and contempt. Martial, more than a century before Christ, in an epigram written to put contempt on one Bassa, who smells ill to the satirist, and whose ill odour he compares to all the fetid exhalations he can think of, counts a Jew's breath worst.

> Quod siccæ redolet palus lacunæ
> . . . . . .
> Quod jejunia Sabbatariorum
> Mæstorum quod anhelitus reorum
> . . . . . .
> Mallem, quam quod oles, olere Bassa.

What stench exhales from an exhausted puddle . . . what evil scent from fasting Sabbatarians . . . . . what belching breath from starving criminals. . . . I would rather smell of them than smell as thou dost, Bassa.* The point of this unclean jest lies in a vulgar mistake that the Jews fasted on a Sabbath, which they certainly did not if they could help it. The same notion of Sabbath fasting appears here and there in satirists, until it is taken up by the historians. So Justin tells, with the air of one who thinks himself well informed, that " Moses, having set out on return to his old country of " Damascus, took his station on Mount Sina, and being, " with his people, wearied after a week's fasting during a " march in the desert of Arabia, consecrated the seventh day " for ever to fasting, which fasting, according to the custom " of his nation, he called *sabbatum*, because that (seventh) day " had made an end of their hunger and their wandering."† This is contrary to every fact of Hebrew history and custom, and to the unanimous agreement of Ezra, Nehemiah, and the

---

* Martialis Epigrammatum, lib. iv. 4.
† Justini Historiarum, lib. xxxvi., cap. 2.

fathers of tradition. They all discountenance dejection and prohibit fasting on the day which was made for us, that we might rejoice in it and be glad. But the Pagans could only look on the Jews and their devotions with contemptuous pity. In their pictures of the Jew you see him pallid with hunger, and he looks as if his lips were moving in silent prayer.* Even the kings go barefoot in the scanty Sabbath feast—for such a feast there must be, after all—and their antiquated clemency spares the aged swine.† They would fain make it appear that the Jew, in his generation, is impoverished by the piety of his fathers, who robbed his life of the light, the enjoyment, and the earnings of every seventh day.‡ His misfortune, it is intimated, was to have a father who feared the Sabbath—*metuentem sabbata patrem*—and bequeathed idleness and poverty to his offspring, as a doleful sign of distinction.

Tacitus and Pliny, somewhat less unfair, are scarcely less mistaken. The latter speaks of the vile and vulgar Jews, a people notable for their contumely of the gods. § He barely notices their existence in his voluminous intelligence of persons and things within the compass of the whole known world, except that he speaks of a river of Judæa that is dry on every Sabbath, ‖ thus repeating the fable of the river *Sambation*. Tacitus does endeavour to be more exact, but

---

* Labra moves tacitus, recutitaque sabbata palles.
   PERSII, Sat. v. 184.

† Observant ubi festa mero pede sabbata reges,
   Et vetus indulget senibus dementia porcis.
   JUVENALIS, Sat. vi. 159, 160.

‡ Sed pater in causa, cui septima quæque fuit lux
   Ignava, et partem vitae non attigit ullam.
   JUVENALIS, Sat. xiv. 105, 106

§ Plinii Hist. Nat., xiii. 9.   ‖ Plinii xxxi. 18.

he very imperfectly succeeds. He tells the same sorry tale of poverty and idleness, but their consecration of the seventh day he attributes to a veneration for the god Saturnus, to whom the Romans dedicate the day which bears his name.* But this historian has not the key to the mystery, nor, if he had, would he have been likely to trace weeks back to their source in the Creation, as known to Moses.

More extended reference to Gentile sources would be tedious. This is enough to show that the Jews' observance of the Sabbath distinguished them from all other nations, but also that it lacked those brighter features which it had sometimes presented, by which it is known to us, and in which they and we shall rejoice together when the Lord of the Sabbath has established his kingdom over all the world.

---

* Taciti Historiarum, lib. v.

CHAPTER IX.

OUR LORD'S MINISTRATIONS ON THE SABBATH-DAY.

THE Lord of the Sabbath-day employed it in miracles of mercy. After the conversation with the Pharisees concerning the ears of corn, He went into a synagogue, "and behold, " there was a man which had his hand withered." (Matt. xii. 10.) We may well conceive that the withered hand attracted his attention, for it was an object far more likely for him to notice than the ostentatious devotions of those mantled hypocrites who, for a pretence, made long prayers. Intent on mischief, the Pharisees asked him, "Is it lawful to " heal on the Sabbath-days? that they might accuse him." They knew that the Sanhedrim would condemn any one who should say that it was lawful so to do. It is not easy to determine how far the traditionists were agreed on that matter; but if they admitted the decision that peril of life drives away the Sabbath, but that it was not lawful to heal a disease that did not endanger life, their answer in a case of withered hand would be that the patient should wait for healing until another day. We may suppose that a withered limb, if by *withered* is meant *palsied*, would not be painful, however inconvenient. There was no agony of pain to be assuaged, nor did any eating gangrene threaten an immediate loss of limb, much less loss of life.

Various Talmudic sentences are quoted to illustrate the principle implied in that question. It was said that if the patient had ear-ache, and applied for relief, the wise men would hold a consultation over him, and according to the apparent measure of his suffering, or the degree of their pity or their favour, they would determine on the probability or improbability of danger, and decide accordingly. "Let not those that are in health," they said, "use medicine on the Sabbath-day. Let not him that labours under a pain in his loins anoint the place with oil and vinegar; but with oil he may, so it be not oil of roses. He that has toothache, let him not take vinegar to spit it out again; but he may swallow it down. Let no man chew mastich, or rub his teeth with spice for a cure; but if he does it to make his mouth sweet, it is allowed. They do not put wine into a sore eye. They do not apply a fomentation or oils to the place affected." These instances may serve to show how far the Pharisaic notions were carried in course of time; but, although they are quoted by eminent commentators,* I could not affirm that in the time of our Lord they had carried their notions to the full extent of such a trivial excess.

With all their nicety as to their fellow-men, they were careful to allow themselves licence enough in managing their cattle. Cattle, being the property of Israelites, were of special value, and were therefore specially privileged. If a sheep fell into a ditch on the Sabbath-day, its owner would lift it out. "How much better, then," said He, "is a man than a sheep? Wherefore it is lawful to do well on the Sabbath-days." That was his decision, whatever the house of Hillel might have determined when deciding in another sense. Accordingly He used his sovereign authority, and not leaving them a moment's space for cavilling, he said to the man, "Stretch forth thine hand. And he stretched it forth; and it was restored whole, like as the other." Struck dumb by the instantaneous miracle, they slank out of his presence, but murmured on the

---

* Lightfoot and Schoettgen.

way, and forthwith took counsel together how they might take his life. But the Lord of the Sabbath remained untouched in plenitude of power; multitudes followed him, and He healed them all. (Matt. xii. 9—15.)

After He had been driven from the synagogue of Nazareth, He came to Capernaum, and taught there on the Sabbath-days. A Galilean Jew, possessed with an unclean spirit, raved madly, bade him let him and the spirit alone, saying " What have we to do with thee, Jesus of Nazareth, art thou " come to destroy us? I know thee who thou art, the Holy " One of God." Jesus rebuked the spirit, and cast it out. The congregation were amazed, and his fame spread over all the country. On the same day, not confining his mercy to the synagogue, He went into Simon's house, and finding Simon's wife's mother ill of a fever, He rebuked the fever, as He would rebuke the storm, and it left her, and immediately she arose, and ministered unto him. (Luke iv. 31—39.)

While teaching in one of the synagogues on the Sabbath, it pleased him to exemplify his power and goodness by laying his hands on an afflicted women who had had a spirit of infirmity eighteen years, was bowed together, and could not stand erect. Immediately she was made whole, and glorified God. The ruler of the synagogue, indignant that the good work should have been done on the Sabbath-day, "said unto the " people, There are six days in which men ought to work; in " them, therefore, come and be healed, and not on the " Sabbath-day. The Lord then answered him, and said, Thou " hypocrite, doth not each one of you on the Sabbath loose " his ox or his ass from the stall, and lead him away to " watering?" There were special provisions that so it should be done, as I have shown in a former chapter. " And ought " not this woman, whom Satan hath bound, lo, these eighteen " years, be loosed from this bond on the Sabbath-day?" The result of this declaration of Sabbath duty was that his adversaries were ashamed, and all the people rejoiced for the glorious things that were done by him. (Luke xiii. 10—17.)

Passing from synagogues, we find our Saviour prosecuting his holy Sabbatic work in the homes of his people.

There is nothing like penance in the Sabbath-keeping of the Bible, at the same time that there is no approach to thoughtless mirth or self-indulgent epicurism. Nehemiah, with all his magisterial severity, when such severity was needful, encouraged his subjects in the enjoyment of innocent domestic comforts. This is manifest on the face of history. Ezra the priest had been reading the Law from the morning until mid-day before a great multitude of men and women in an open place of the city, and the service was exceeding solemn. It was, with anticipation of five hundred years, almost a picture of the grand assemblies held by apostles and apostolic men, first in that same Jerusalem, and then in other chief cities of the world. The people had stood, hour after hour, in deep attention, drinking in the words with closest self-application. When the priest blessed the Lord, the great multitude answered " Amen, amen," with uplifted hands, as taking God to witness. And then they bowed their heads in silence. The Levites were not yet ready to hold a choral service. The citizens had not yet put off the sorrows of a remorseful penitence, and when the history of their nation was recited, and God's long-despised Law was once more published, they wept as people sometimes weep when faithful ministers of God's truth cause them to understand the reading : " All the people " wept when they heard the words of the law." " And " Nehemiah, which is the Tirshatha [or governor], and " Ezra the priest the scribe, and the Levites that taught " the people, said unto all the people, This day is holy unto " the Lord your God ; mourn not, nor weep. . . . Go your

G

"way, eat the fat, and drink the sweet, and send portions
"unto them for whom nothing is prepared: for this day
"is holy unto our Lord: neither be ye sorry; for the joy
"of the Lord is your strength." That day was the new moon, but it was holy, as is the Sabbath, and because the day was holy, the people were to honour it by eating their food with gladness. (Nehem. viii. 1—12.) For this reason the more wealthy Jews, in the time of our Lord, made Sabbath-feasts, not only as a matter of indulgence, but of sacred hospitality, with a mingling of religious feeling, real or professed.

On that best of days, soon as the sun had set, and the last moment of common time expired, they made a cheerful meal of choicest meats. The hurry and fag of preparation was not permitted to break in upon the comfort of consecrated hours. There was not a trace of confusion—not a speck of dust. Every garment was clean and every face happy, unless some sharp disease or sudden grief had come to "drive away the "Sabbath." Pleasure, or traffic, or aggressive war, might never drive it away, and therefore man's will might not be gratified to the violation of God's ordinance. The Sabbath-feast was gladsome indeed, yet holy, and a priest or a wise man was usually present to pronounce a blessing, and to lead the conversation of the company. Therefore Jesus of Nazareth was sometimes—often, perhaps—bidden to the feast that He might honour and bless the house.

St. Luke narrates one of those visits. He writes that our Lord went to the house of one of the chief Pharisees "to eat bread on the Sabbath-day, and they"—that is, the Pharisees—"*were lying wait for him,*" ἦσαν παρατηρούμενοι αὐτόν. The occasion of their lying wait was, no doubt, their dislike of his teaching, and his conduct also in respect of the Sabbath. From the whole tenor of the narrative it is apparent that the party consisted of persons of rank and wealth, and that the number of invited guests was large. Among the guests there was one very unlikely person to be in such a place, unless he had been carried thither for a special purpose. He could not have come without help, and they who brought him did not seem to have brought him to be healed, for they made no prayer on his behalf. Certainly he was not one of the household, or when healed and enabled to move, it would not be said that Jesus *let him go*, ἀπέλυσε. " Jesus answering"—pursuing in words the thoughts of their hearts, which were to him as intelligible as uttered voice—" spake unto the lawyers and Pharisees"—who are with reason supposed to have brought the man thither with the design of raising the very question, " Is it lawful to " heal on the Sabbath-day?" They were evidently taken by surprise, as well they might be, if conscious of detection in a plot, and, like men smitten with confusion, held their peace. Answering the question for himself, he took the dropsical man, healed him, and let him go.

Still they were silent. The rapidity of discourse and the suddenness of miracle had sealed their lips, and left them without power of reply, while He pleaded with them on the ground of mere humanity, and turned against themselves their own interpretation of the Law. " Which of you shall " have an ass or an ox fallen into a pit, and will not straight- " way pull him out on the Sabbath-day? And they could " not answer him again to these things." If the ultimate decision of the Talmudists is that healing on that day was not lawful—except under strict limitations—it surely had the majority of casuists in its favour.

No controversy followed, nor any accusation of having broken the Law, but He immediately proceeded to instruct them in humility, and to inculcate charity and condescension, delivering the parable of the Great Supper, which foreshadows the Gospel Feast, and provides the ministers of the Gospel with one of the finest themes of evangelical appeal. (Luke xiv. 1—24.)

Last of all, I would refer to the fifth chapter of the Gospel according to St. John for an exposition of the Sabbath in its relation to Christ himself, and therefore under its most important aspect to us Christians.

Jesus went up to Jerusalem at a feast of the Jews. While in the city, He went to Bethesda—*House of Mercy*. It was a building, or pile of buildings, with five porches opening on a pool, which was stirred at certain seasons by the descent of an angel. " Whosoever then first after the troubling of the " water stepped in was made whole of whatsoever disease he " had." One poor man, utterly helpless, had lain there thirty-eight years, and witnessed the healing of many; but long before he could creep to the edge of the pool, another was sure to step down before him. The water was not then moved, and therefore whatever miracle of healing might be wrought in Bethesda that day would not be attributed to the visitation of an angel. " Jesus said unto him, Rise, take up " thy bed, and walk. Immediately the man was made whole, " and took up his bed, and walked : and on the same day was " the Sabbath." Now, it would have been difficult for the Pharisees, even on their own principles, to establish against Jesus the charge of breaking any law. He had not anointed the man. He had not so much as stretched out his hand to lift him up. Speaking is not one of the thirty-nine primary works, and He had only spoken. The saying " Take up thy bed and walk" could not have made him guilty according to any canon of Jewish tradition that I have ever heard of. It was the man himself who committed what they would call a breach of law, by carrying his bed; whereas they would have held any one guilty for carrying a straw or a feather. The man, then, broke their law, but threw the blame on him that healed him. "The Jews therefore persecuted Jesus, and "sought to slay him, because He had done these things on "the Sabbath-day.

"But Jesus answered them, *My Father worketh hitherto,* "*and I work.*" By calling God his Father, He certainly made himself of the same nature, and therefore in so far equal with God; and this being considered blasphemy, which was a far more heinous offence than even Sabbath-breaking, their dispute was turned into another channel, and we are left to interpret the sentence as he spoke it.

"Hitherto," or *until now,* ἕως ἄρτι, could not refer to the work of creation, from which God ceased after the six days, but to that work from which He never ceases; and that never-ceasing work, as a Hebrew commentator truly and beautifully says, *is goodness.* (Ps. xxxi. 19.) This divine and ceaseless work the Father of All began to do in Paradise on the first Sabbath-day. Ever since that beginning there had been one day of every seven wherein sacred works only might be done lawfully. Such a work as circumcision, with the pain attending, and the delicately careful treatment necessary, was not light. The same was to be said of the New Moon sacrifices. Whenever they occurred, it was no trifling work to offer them, but the work was done on the Sabbath-day, being God's work; it was done for him, and Sabbath could not be broken by the priest in offering them. This, however, was not what our Lord intended to insist upon, for He doubtless meant to affirm that whatever work He did was in the very fact divine; that his works of mercy were absolutely the same in kind as his Father's works of perpetual goodness. He did no more than He saw his Father do, but his works were done visibly in the sight of men. He preached the glad tidings of release and liberty. He taught sacred truths with a laborious activity, exposing himself to perils utterly repellent of self-indulgence, and making repose impossible. He actively sought out the afflicted; He visited and healed the sick. What the Pharisees thanklessly looked upon as a material action, was with him a moral, nay, a godlike act. Such it would be if, without miracle, and by the use of ordinary means, it were done by any of his servants. Not only so: whatever He did, it became their duty to do also, if by ordinary means and with God's blessing it could be accomplished, for He gave them an example that they should walk in his steps. Miracles we cannot do on any day, and at the line which divides the miraculous from the natural our duty stops.

I cannot refrain from translating a paraphrase of the words of our Lord, written by Nicholas Zeger, a Minorite friar of the sixteenth century; too good to be rejected because a friar wrote them. Would that friars had written much more so excellent, and then there would have been fewer of their fraternities in the world.

"*My Father worketh hitherto, and I work.* If you ask how
" my Father has been working onward to this very time,
" although it is written that on the seventh day God rested
" from all his works that He had made, you have only to
" look around and see in what good order all things consist,
" how they are governed, and how they are renewed, and you
" will understand what is meant by the perpetual working of
" my Father. When I say, then, that my Father has been
" working until now, and that I work, it is as if I should say
" that as my Father, after those six days of creation wrought
" also in that Sabbath of his which even yet continues, and
" ceases not from his work of universal government, whereby
" He produces a continual succession of things, like from like,
" in which he is every day busied, without ceasing from

"bestowing benefits on men; so I, who am his Son, having received from him both the will and the power to do what is necessary for the salvation of mankind, am not hindered by the sanctity of the Sabbath from doing whatever my Father requires of me."

Barely to say that God is so essentially active that He cannot cease from working, any more than cold could cease to freeze, or fire to burn, is a gross and insufficient illustration. Philo, the Jew, speaks thus, but we need not recite his saying. The words of our Lord Jesus to the Pharisees cannot signify less than I have endeavoured to point out. He had come to enter on his kingdom; and, as our King and God, it pleased him to have a Sabbath for himself, a Sabbath adorned and sanctified with goodness, a day when men should leave their own works, and occupy themselves in doing their Master's business, and showing forth their Master's glory.

CHAPTER X.

THE LORD'S DAY, OR CHRISTIAN SABBATH.

On the sixth day of the week our Blessed Lord was crucified. At the third hour he was nailed to the cross. At the sixth hour an awful darkness overspread the heavens, and continued until the ninth, when He yielded up his life, and the sun shone out again. From the ninth hour to the twelfth was the Preparation for the Sabbath, and in that interval Joseph of Arimathea went to Pilate to beg the body, took it down from the cross, and before sunset he had laid it in his own sepulchre. Then the Sabbath-lamps were lit.

The hours of the Preparation must have been fully occupied by the disciples, not in preparing their dwellings for the Sabbath meal, but in providing costly spices and ointment for the embalming. To them, therefore, the once consecrated hour came without the needful preparation, and all the hours of that holy day were spent in mourning. They kept an involuntary fast, and the silence of death reigned within the tomb of the Arimathean, wherein no man had hitherto been laid. Again the sun went down, and the eve of the first day of another week began. The guards were still watching round the sealed sepulchre, and the disciples, suspected of an intention to steal the body while men slept, waited for morning before they would venture to approach; but with the morning star they came.

Yet earlier than they, a mighty angel flashing with glory came down from heaven, rolled away the stone from the mouth of the sepulchre, and saluted his immortal Master as He rose from the stony bed, and came forth untouched by the taint of death. The stricken guards forsook their post, and the earliest day-dawn lighted the disciples to the place where they thought their Lord was laid.

The evening was past and the morning come, and again, at the commencement of a New Creation, as the regeneration of a lost world began, it might, with double truth, be said, that the evening and the morning were the first day.

With the Saviour's crucifixion ceased his Sabbath visits to the synagogues, and with his resurrection began another custom. On that last of undisputed "days of Sabbath" Jerusalem shows signs of sad amazement, if not of ceremonial mourning. If men did not wear sackcloth and cast ashes on their heads, they were dumb in wonder and beating their breasts in penitence. Wherever they went, while listening to the choir in the Temple, or to the blessings pronounced over the wine and the bread of the hastily-prepared Sabbath-meal, one sentence, pronounced amidst the departing shadows of a preternatural eclipse, resounded in their ears—*Truly this was a righteous man.*

The Christian reader needs not now a recital of the wonders which distinguished that first Lord's-day. No command was given, but, before the second day of the week came, joys greater than the joys of Sabbath were imparted to the disciples. From the moment when the angel said to the disciples that entered the vacated tomb, "He is not here, but He is risen"—from that moment the entire course of Christian history was fashioned. Days began to take new names, and a series of such happy and blessed Sabbaths as the world had never known was now begun.

Let us carefully mark the first of them, and the few that followed thereupon, and we shall certainly find that the change of Sabbath rest and worship from the seventh day to the first was neither arbitrary nor accidental. We may, however, digress for a moment to observe that, after all, it is not possible to prove that the seventh day of the week was indeed the seventh counting from the day of the first Sabbath in Paradise; and every one who gives a moment's consideration on this point must see that such a calculation was impossible, and that even if it were possible it is immaterial. It would have been immeasurably more natural for the sons of Noah to have counted from the first day of entering the Ark, or from the day of the covenant by sacrifice after quitting it, than for them to have laboured, without record or monument to help them, to cross trackless wastes of time without a single waymark left upon them—ages of enforced abstinence from the great benefit of seventh-days' rest, when not even household memory remained to guide them.

A conversation, which took place between two eminent Jews in the tenth century of our era, contains observations made by each of them well worth remembering. Saadiah was an enthusiastic devotee of Talmudical tradition, and maintained the insufficiency of Holy Scripture to tell us all things needful to be known. Ben Yerukhim was a Karaite, who maintained just the contrary, and professed entire contentment with God's written law. Among other pleas for the necessity of tradition, Saadiah made this, that "no one knows how to "count the seventh day from the Creation, nor can any one "tell when the Sabbath ought to fall, the law being silent on "that matter." Ben Yerukhim allows this fully, but does not acknowledge any difficulty in the matter, and answers the eminent traditionist in few words: "Every person in every "place well knows that already."* Both these men agree that it is not known when the seventh day from the Creation falls, but the Karaite, whose manner of keeping the Sabbath is far

---

* Rule's History of the Karaite Jews. Chap. xii.

the stricter of the two, considers that to follow the present custom in that respect is quite sufficient to satisfy the intention of the law.

If any verbal command was given to change the Sabbath-day, there is no record of it; yet the change was never disputed, so far as we know, but it was evidently consistent with the will of Christ; and although there is no contemporaneous Jewish writing bearing reference to the fact, so far as I am myself informed—and I abstain from searching so late writings as the Talmudic tractates—yet I may mention that Lightfoot, quotes from one such writing in the *Abodah Zárah,* where the *Lord's Day* is mentioned as the *Christian Day,* יום נוצרי, and the name Nazarene, or Christian, is defined as designating one of the followers of the Man *who commanded* that the first day of the week should be made a holy day for them. * Now, although the Talmud is not admissible as an authority with us, and therefore could not be honestly insisted on by us in an argument with Jews, we may, nevertheless, attach some consideration to the fact that, in a remote century of our era, it was believed by the chief antagonists of Christianity that Christ had *commanded* the first day of the week to be their holy day. If nothing more, it is the historical note of an opinion.

In the absence of direct evidence of an express command, we glean from the New Testament enough to show what must have been his will in this respect, and will now anticipate the result by calling the first day of the week *The Lord's Day,* by which name the Resurrection-day will be henceforth distinguished. Our Lord appeared to his disciples no less than four times on the day of his rising from the grave.

First—to the women whom He met, saying, "All hail!

---

* Lightfoot's Hebrew and Talmudical Exercitations on Matt. xxviii. 1.

"And they came and held him by the feet, and worshipped him." (Matt. xxviii. 9.)

Second—to St. Peter. (Luke xxiv. 12—34.)

Third—to the two disciples whom He met on the way to Emmaus, with whom he conversed, expounding to them in all the Scriptures the things concerning himself, and to whom he made himself known in the breaking of bread, while their hearts burned within them. (Luke xxiv. 13—32.

Fourth—in Jerusalem, at a later hour of the same day, if now we may include that later hour in the twenty-four of the first day, seeing that with the dawn began the knowledge of his resurrection, and the notation of the hours. The Hebrew division of days gives place to the Roman, and time is to be counted in keeping with the Gentile usage. At Emmaus, when he had vanished out of their sight, the two disciples "rose up the same hour, and returned to Jerusalem, and found the eleven gathered together, and them that were with them, saying, The Lord is risen indeed, and hath appeared to Simon. And they told what things were done in the way, and how He was known of them in breaking of bread. And as they thus spake, Jesus himself stood in the midst of them, and saith unto them, Peace be unto you." (Luke xxiv. 33—36.) Again, for the second time the same day, the Lord gave them a full exposition of what is written concerning himself in the Law, the Prophets, and the Psalms. Again He opened their understanding, that they might understand the Scriptures. Again, by his own act and example, He instructed them how the same holy writings were to be expounded, and how they should minister the Gospel of Salvation—"that repentance and remission of sins should be preached in his name among all nations, beginning at Jerusalem." (v. 47.)

So special is the character of these discourses, that we must pause to consider why they were not given before this day, and why they are *now* given. On this day He that was dead is alive—has appeared first in his character as the Lamb of God, sacrificed to make atonement for the sins of men. Before this day it could not have been said that the prophetic Scriptures relating to the Atonement were fulfilled. But on this day it can be so declared, and the disciples may not close their eyes in sleep until they have been fully instructed in the fact, and so far prepared to bear witness of it to the world.

Now let us pause and think.

Is it likely that, after having set aside the observance of the Sabbath on the seventh day, the day on which it always had been kept, and having even changed, if we understand the text of St. Luke aright, the order of the day's beginning, the Lord of the Sabbath would with so great solemnity and care set apart that very day after his resurrection for preparing his disciples for their work, and for the work that should engage the energies of their successors through future ages, and yet throw aside the institution which had been the means of preserving some knowledge of God in the world by reading in synagogues the Scriptures which He then expounded, and then commanded his disciples to publish in all nations?

After such a consecration of every moment of that first day of Christian history, in so close resemblance to the sanctification of the first day in the history of mankind, is it credible that He who thus began to plant the second Paradise should at the same time set aside the Sabbath, and leave to a so-called Christian liberty the fatal freedom to exchange the holy rest and blessedness of God's own day for a licence to go on erring from his ways and wandering in selfishness unblest? Nay, rather let us confess that this is the day which He made for himself, that we might rejoice in it and be glad.

We must not fail to observe that on that same day He

commissioned his disciples to preach the Gospel to the world. It was in the memorable conversation which then took place in Jerusalem that He gave them their commission. "The same day at evening, being the first day of the week, when the doors were shut where the disciples were assembled for fear of the Jews, came Jesus and stood in the midst, and saith unto them, Peace be unto you. And when He had so said, He showed unto them his hands and his side. Then were the disciples glad, when they saw the Lord. Then said Jesus to them again, Peace be unto you: as my Father hath sent me, even so send I you. And when He had said this, He breathed on them, and saith unto them, Receive ye the Holy Ghost: Whose soever sins ye remit, they are remitted unto them; and whose soever sins ye retain, they are retained." (John xx. 19—23.)* The true meaning of these words, as I humbly believe, the reader will see in the footnote. Thus understood, they show that on the first Lord's-day provision was made for the canon of revealed Christian truth, and for the establishment of the Christian ministry, and that power was then conveyed to the real fathers of the Christian Church for the effectual discharge of the duties of their most sacred, peculiar, and intransferable office.

With all this we have not yet enough to establish our position, which is, that, after failing to keep the Sabbath as a Sabbath ought to be kept on the seventh day, while Jesus lay in

---

* I cannot conveniently digress from our present subject to enter into a controversy with those who believe that these words of Christ convey to priests a power to forgive sins. They have nothing to do with any but the Apostles. To them our Lord conveyed power and authority, by the inspiration of the Holy Ghost, to lay down the law of Christ's kingdom in the world, and to give infallible direction concerning the way of salvation by the remission of sins.

the sepulchre, Sabbath was really kept on the day of Resurrection, and that the first day of the week, like the first of time, was thenceforth to be the Sabbath-day for the Christian world. If the sacred narrative threw no further light on the subject, it would become us to confess that the seventh day, for aught we knew to the contrary, might still be the Sabbath-day. The question being in that case still doubtful, it would be our duty to leave it so until further information could be found in the writings of those holy men who received the keys of unfailing knowledge from their Master's hand. But if the solemnities of that first Lord's-day are found to be but first in a weekly succession of like events, and if the New Testament contains further intimations entirely consistent with the conviction of Christians of all ages that such a change of day was then confirmed, we shall not have to set about another labour that would be severely difficult indeed—the labour of quenching an intimate conviction, setting at nought evidences received as clear and indisputable, and disputing a supreme authority. But the solemnities of the first day of the first Christian week were eminently Sabbatic, and the desired confirmation was actually given. We know what took place on that day week.

"After eight days again his disciples were within, and " Thomas with them: then came Jesus, and stood in the " midst, and said, Peace be unto you." On this followed the assurance of Thomas that the Lord had indeed risen, and the one disciple who had not been present with his brethren the week before, now sees the proofs that this is really the risen Saviour, and acknowledges him to be his " Lord and his God." (John xx. 24—29.) This gives us two successive Lord's-days, which were marked and hallowed by the assemblage of Christ with his disciples after his resurrection from the dead. For, be it noted, that *after eight* days, μεθ' ἡμέρας ὀκτὼ, is equivalent with the English *on that day week*. Other languages would be idiomatically the same as the Greek; as in the Spanish, for example, they say, *al cabo de ocho dias*.

There were yet four more first days of the weeks before our Lord's ascension, of which there is no note of any further meeting between him and his disciples. It is not said on what day He appeared to them at the Sea of Tiberias, which appearance is called *the third*. We may presume, however, that it was not on the seventh day, or they would not have been fishing. The most natural conjecture is that it pleased our Lord to meet them on a working day, and to bestow on them a signal blessing amidst their ordinary labours for a livelihood, at the same time urging them onward, and cheering them with heavenly discourse. Neither is the day of the Ascension numbered, unless its being forty days *after* the Resurrection means that there were forty exclusive of the Resurrection and Ascension days themselves; but that is not likely. Conjectures have not the force of evidence, and as the Gospels have not the form of diaries, their silence on this matter is not of the least importance.

Concerning the day of Pentecost there can be no doubt, for it is the Feast of Weeks. On Thursday, 14th Nisan (Lev. xxiii. 5), Jesus and his disciples ate the paschal supper. (Mark xiv. 12.) On Friday, first day of unleavened bread, when they killed the passover, was the Crucifixion. On Sunday, the Resurrection. That Sunday—we now use the Roman names of days—was the morrow after the Sabbath, the day appointed by the Mosaic law for the Feast of Pentecost. " Ye shall count unto you *from the morrow after the* " *Sabbath*, from the day that ye brought the sheaf of the wave " offering; seven Sabbaths shall be complete. Even unto " *the morrow after the seventh Sabbath* shall ye number *fifty* "*days;* and ye shall offer a new meat-offering unto the "Lord." (Lev. xxiii. 15—16.) Without question, therefore, the day of Pentecost fell on a Sunday.

"And when the day of Pentecost was fully come, they "were all with one accord in one place." (Acts ii. 1.) They had been assembled in an upper room, and were continuing in one accord with prayer and supplication, waiting to receive power by the Holy Ghost which should be poured out upon them; waiting to receive instruction touching matters of pressing importance for that time. There, also, they had prayed for guidance in the election of a successor to Judas Iscariot, the traitor; and there they cast the lots, and found Matthias to be chosen. Not on the Sabbath-day as the Jews held it, and when the sacred assemblies were holden in the synagogues, but on the morrow after the accustomed Sabbath the Holy Spirit, which Christ had promised, came down on them from heaven.

Thus again was the Divine presence manifested in an exclusively Christian assemblage on the first day of the week, with majesty and power surpassing all that had ever been experienced. It was, in fact, the eighth Sunday whereon the Christians kept Sabbath after a new manner, not only ceasing from their daily work, but consecrating the day to God with solemnities such as the law of Moses did not provide. What their conduct was in regard to the ancient seventh-day Sabbath, we shall consider presently. It suffices to note here that on the morning of the first Lord's day they saw the risen Saviour, and on the morning of the eighth they saw the heavenly flames which attested his mighty presence in their midst again.

This glorious day was consecrated to the preaching of the Gospel, not in words of man's wisdom, but words which the Holy Ghost teacheth. The Divine Paraclete had come, and the preachers spake under his resistless impulse. The proclamation of the Gospel was made in Jerusalem, it is true, but not in "the holy language," as the Jews called the Hebrew, hallowed by the lips of prophets—not in that language in which the restorers of Jerusalem, after the captivity, first read the law, and after the reading interpreted the sentences into the vernacular. Far different was it now. The message of gladness was delivered in many Gentile dialects. Every man heard it plainly spoken in his own mother-tongue. So was the day consecrated for this blessed ministration in all the languages that men then spake, or ever shall speak.

The Apostles are now permitted to leave Jerusalem, and proceed on their mission to the world. They are empowered to preach the Gospel to every creature, that is to say, to all the Gentiles.* Now they can bear witness of the grace of God in Christ, and lay the foundations far and wide of a church large enough to comprehend all nations under heaven. Armed with special authority, accredited with extraordinary powers, and guided by the spirit of unerring truth and wisdom, they originated the few institutions necessary for the formation and maintenance of Christian congregations.

For the express purpose of instructing their Hebrew brethren, they frequented the synagogues on the Sabbath days, honouring the primeval institutions. From week to week they are to be found in the synagogues. So Barnabas and Paul, separated to their work and sent forth by the Holy Ghost, depart from Antioch, set sail from Seleucia, and land in Cyprus. Then they preach the word of God in Salamis in the synagogues of the Jews, go through the isle unto Paphos, and, having preached Christ to Sergius Paulus and con-

---

* Πάσῃ τῇ κτίσει—לכל הבריות.

founded the sorceror, they loose from Paphos, come to Perga in Pamphylia, and thence to Antioch in Pisidia. Here they go into the synagogue on the Sabbath-day, and sit down to teach. After a memorable discourse by St. Paul, the Jews, being hardened, leave the synagogue, and the Gentiles who are present beseech that those words may be preached to them the next Sabbath; "and the next Sabbath-day came "almost the whole city together to hear the word of God."*

The same course of ministration they pursued after their return to Antioch. It was on the Sabbath that they went into the oratory by the river-side at Philippi, and Lydia was converted to Christianity (Acts xvi. 13.) At Thessalonica, St. Paul, "as his manner was," went into the synagogue, "and three Sabbath-days reasoned with them out of the "Scriptures." (Acts xvii. 1, 2.) At Corinth, again, he reasoned in the synagogue every Sabbath, and persuaded both Jews and Greeks. (Acts xviii. 4.) So at Ephesus (xix. 8), speaking boldly for the space of three months.

Christianity was not yet established in any of these places, and as there was not Christian worship, there could not yet be any Christian Sabbath, but that would surely follow in due time. At their first entrance into Jewish populations they joined their Hebrew brethren on the old Sabbath, not raising any question as to its nature, which was well enough understood; nor needlessly concerning themselves about the number, first or seventh, of the day for its observance, so it were observed faithfully. But it soon appeared that the first day was in fact marked for consecration to Christian worship and instruction, however much the seventh might supply occasions for preaching the Gospel to the Jews. To Jews and Gentiles alike they proclaimed " Jesus and the Resurrec-

---

* Acts xiii., xiv.

"tion," but it was to the latter that they most diligently insisted on the doctrine of resurrection from the dead in congregations assembled on the Resurrection-day.

So much might be inferred from an incident in the narrative of St. Paul's return from Greece to Palestine, where St. Luke, his companion, describes their brief sojourn at Troas. " We sailed away from Philippi after the days of unleavened " bread, and came unto them in Troas, where we abode seven " days." Now in those seven days the Apostle could not fail to show his accustomed reverence to the Sabbath as observed by his Jewish brethren, unless some unrecorded circumstance, or some personal reason to the contrary unknown to history, or a contrary custom established by Christianity, should induce him to act otherwise. Whether or not, it is certain that, in that full week of days, a Saturday and Sunday, so to speak, could not but occur. The latter of the two is mentioned by the narrator: " Upon the first day of the " week, when the disciples came together to break bread, " Paul preached unto them, ready to depart on the morrow; " and continued his speech until midnight. And there were " many lights in the upper chamber, where they were gathered " together." (Acts xx. 6, 8.)

Now it cannot be understood that the congregation in the upper chamber at Troas, not probably the room used as a synagogue at other times, was convened merely on occasion of St. Paul's departure, which was expected to take place on the morrow, the second day of the week, for it is said that they came together *to break bread*, or as the Peshito Syriac renders it, *that we might break the Eucharist*, דְּנֶקְצָא אוּכָרְסְיָא. A eucharistic service would scarcely be permitted in a synagogue, and it is therefore most probable, if not quite evident, that the Troad Christians had a separate place of assemblage, an upper room prepared, and many lights in it, a precaution obviously necessary, that there might be full publicity, and no unseemly appearance of obscurity. Thus provided with many lights, all the congregation might be able to read the Holy Scriptures of the Old Testament, with, perhaps, such treatises or narratives as St. Luke himself refers to in another place. (Luke i. 1, 4.) Or, when thus assembled, they might have occasion to inspect the letters of commendation presented by Christian strangers come to Troas from distant congregations (2 Cor. iii. 1), agreeably to a similar custom observed in synagogues. (Acts xxii. 5.) It can scarcely be possible to doubt that this describes an established Christian congregation, habitually assembling on the first day of the week. Such an arrangement would naturally take place as soon as even two or three were separated from the synagogue, "cast out" because of faith in Christ. They would certainly meet together in the name of Christ, and would enjoy his presence in their midst.

Very soon we find direct allusions to such regular Sunday services addressed to the ruder congregations of Galatia and the more pretentious society of Corinth. Take the few words following, addressed by St. Paul to the Corinthians. "Now "concerning the collection for the saints, as I have given "order to the churches of Galatia, even so do ye. Upon the "first day of the week let every one of you lay by him in "store, as God hath prospered him, that there be no gather- "ings when I come." (1 Cor. xvi. 1, 2.) By these instances we perceive that the Law of Moses could have been preserved in Babylonia, as well as in Greece or Lesser Asia, without a confessor, and the knowledge of that Law in Persia or in Italy without synagogues, or as easily could there have been a *sign* to distinguish between the families of Jews and Gentiles without a Sabbath, as could the doctrines of Christianity, and a solemn and united approach to God through the mediation of our Lord Jesus Christ, be maintained in the world without a Sabbath-day and Sabbath worship.

So, when the beloved disciple, in hoary age, "was in the "isle that is called Patmos, for the word of God, and for "the testimony of Jesus Christ," he found solace there in the sanctification of a day in the Christian manner. He was "in "the spirit on the Lord's day." (Rev. i. 10.) I think it is universally acknowledged that this was the first day of the week, but "the Lord's day" is so plain and unequivocal a designation that I believe it is literally accepted in all the old versions except one, the Ethiopic, made for the use of a very remote church where the nomenclature of Christendom had scarcely become known, but where the Hebrew style was familiar in its application to all religious subjects. The Greek is made more plain in that version by the substitution of the Hebrew form, *on the first day*.

Here closes the New Testament account of the Christian Sabbath, and with this we might well be satisfied if all Christians were content with the evidence of Holy Scripture. That, however, is not the case; and an historical survey would not be complete which did not assist such readers as have not yet disentangled themselves from the perplexity thrown around the subject to ascertain the causes of this perplexity. This can best be done by observing how Christians treated the matter while the Church was in its infancy, how it came to pass that the weekly sanctification of a day to God fell into inobservance, and how conflicting opinions superseded the happy unanimity of the apostolic age.

Three passages of St. Paul are quoted by those who say that the Sabbath passed away together with the Mosaic ritual.

The apostle wrote to the Galatians (iv. 10, 11): "Ye "observe days, and months, and times, and years. I am "afraid of you, lest I have bestowed among you labour in vain." They suppose that the Galatians observed Sabbath-days, new moons, Hebrew feasts, and Sabbatic years. This is contrary to probability, as well as to the context, where we read that they were heathens before their conversion, and were turning back to idolatry again. They were relapsing into the old pagan folly of calculating lucky and unlucky days and times. Astrology or divination governed their actions. The stars to them were more than God.

To the Jewish converts at Rome he wrote (Rom. xiv. 5): "One man esteemeth one day above another: another esteemeth every day alike. Let every man be fully persuaded in his own mind." This evidently refers to the question constantly occurring when Jews were converted to Christianity. St. Paul would not precipitate the conclusion. The change would certainly be made from the seventh-day Sabbath to the first, but time should be allowed, and freedom left to individuals meanwhile.

Exactly in the same spirit he addressed the Colossians (ii. 16): "Let no man judge you in meat, or in drink, or in respect of a holy day, or of the new moon, or of *Sabbaths* [$\sigma\alpha\beta\beta\acute{\alpha}\tau\omega\nu$] : which are a shadow of things to come ; but the body is of Christ." It was not the institution of the Sabbath that was called in question in Galatia, or at Rome, or at Colossæ. The only question anywhere that had relation to the Sabbath-*day* was, whether it should be the seventh or the first. This was, like other matters that are specified, the *shadow* only ; the *body* is Christ. But that which is the body must have its own shadow.

CHAPTER XI.

THE CHRISTIAN SABBATH IN THE FIRST THREE CENTURIES.

NOTHING can be more distinct than the demarcation of the apocryphal from the divine. There was not any visible wall of separation raised around the mount "that might be "touched," but a barrier of dread effectually guarded every approach; and while within that barrier Moses held communion with the God of glory, outside the line Aaron his brother was making the molten calf. So Paul and Barnabas were close companions, and, for a time, faithful fellow-labourers; yet the writings of these two men—if indeed the epistle attributed to the latter be authentic, and not greatly corrupted—are substantially dissimilar, and fairly represent the difference between Apostles and "Apostolic Fathers." Barnabas is counted first of the fathers, and was once called the fourteenth apostle. Assuredly, he was much unlike the twelve inspired witnesses of Christ then seated on their thrones to judge the twelve tribes of Israel.

Barnabas is said to have written a catholic epistle wherein he speaks of the Sabbath, and, after some quotations from the Old Testament, gives his own interpretation thus: "Attend, my children, to what He says, '*finished in six* "'*days*'—that is to say, in six thousand years. The Lord "God will consummate all things, for with Him the day is "a thousand years, as He himself testifies, saying: 'Behold, "'this day shall be as a thousand years.' (Ps. xc. 4?) "Therefore, children, in six days—that is, in six thousand "years—all things shall be consummated. *And He rested* "*the seventh day*—that is, when his Son shall come and make an end of the time of the wicked one, and shall judge the ungodly, and shall change the sun, and moon, and stars; then shall He rest gloriously in the seventh day. And further He saith, '*Thou shalt sanctify it with clean hands.*' If, then, God sanctified that day, now none can keep it holy, except it be with a heart altogether clean. Therefore, consider that He who rested gloriously will sanctify it when we, having received the righteous promises, there being no more iniquity, shall be able to hallow that day, when all things are made new by the Lord, and we are ourselves first made holy. And, again, he says to them, '*Your new moons and your Sabbaths I cannot away with.*' (Is. i. 13.) Consider how He speaks: the Sabbaths that now are are not acceptable to me; but those which I have made, when having completed all things, I shall make a beginning of the eighth day—that is to say, the beginning of another world. Therefore, we, too, pass the eighth day in rejoicing, wherein Jesus also rose from the dead, and, having appeared openly, ascended into heaven."*

Here is a basis of historic truth, an express recognition of the primeval Sabbath, and a literal quotation from the Decalogue, yet it is followed by a millenarian dream. All the historical and preceptive Scriptures, which have hitherto been treated with sobriety at least, are now explained away, as if the Oriental fables of periods in creation of hundreds or thousands of years were to be adopted in place of the Mosaic account of days. To this end, two or three poetical conceptions of the immutability of God are put in the stead of a practical commandment. Because the Sabbaths polluted with idolatry in the times of the kings of Samaria and

---

* S. Barnabæ Epistolæ, cap. **xv.**

Judah were hateful to God, it is all at once inferred that the Sabbath appointed for all the world in every age was abolished; and the scriptural evidences, which are so familiar to every attentive reader of the Bible, were set aside by this Levite from Cyprus, whose zeal and self-denial had bespoken the reverence of ages, but whose incompetence as a teacher is exhibited in the writing that bears his name. Learned men, whose attention has been fixed so closely on the writings of the Apostolic Fathers for purposes of sacred criticism that it would almost seem presumptuous to differ from them, agree to accept the writing attributed to Barnabas as a "monument of the first Christian age."* The publication in that age of views so extremely unscriptural and wild portends the very departure from apostolical Christianity which eventually took place, and assists us to account for the prevalence in the Christian Church of such notions in relation to the Sabbath as we had not found anywhere until we closed the Old Testament and the New, and took up the mutilated remains of a companion of the great theologian of the primitive Church, who seems permitted to wander in the trackless wilderness of private interpretation that his name and his associations may not bring him so near the standard of inspired Scripture as to confuse the boundaries of human invention and Divine revelation, but to mark them in their true characters, and to throw around Mount Calvary a boundary of supernatural defence as impassable as that which was drawn around Mount Sinai.

About the last year of the first century, or first of the second, Ignatius wrote his epistle to the Magnesians, and, like Barnabas, in his endeavours to dissuade the Magnesian Christians from Jewish customs and opinions, he bids them

---

* Westcott on the Canon of the New Testament, chap. i., sect. 4.

no longer Sabbatize, but live according to the Lord's-day, that is to say, to live consistently with the faith professed and the worship rendered to God on that day, the day whereon our Saviour rose from the dead, who is our life, in whom our life sprang up again, even by his death, whom some deny.*

The teaching of Ignatius, however, is far superior to that of Barnabas, and if by Sabbatizing he means no more than keeping the Sabbath in the Jewish way, as it has been described in a preceding chapter, his teaching is unexceptionable. So understood, it harmonizes perfectly with the tenor of our Lord's doctrine, which he appears to have studied well. Perhaps the zealous and rude Cypriote had not so studied. Yet these two writers equally attest the observance of the Lord's-day as very distinct from a seventh-day Sabbath, and so far their evidence is of equal value as regards the history of the institution, while the discordance of their doctrinal teaching strengthens the force of their historical agreement.

The report of Pliny the Younger, written from Bithynia to the Roman Emperor, has been quoted times without number. He relates that the Christians in that country assembled habitually on a stated day before sunrise, sang a hymn to Christ as God, and bound themselves by an oath not to do anything criminal, that they would not commit thefts, nor robberies, nor adulteries, nor be guilty of any breach of faith or failure to restore a pledge.* The oath, or *sacramentum*, not well understood by the proconsul, was probably the Eucharist, which, although not an oath, had all the force of one on the conscience of the participant.† The sins here enumerated exclude those who commit them from the kingdom

---

* —μηκέτι σαββατίζοντες, ἀλλὰ κατὰ κυριακὴν ἐν ᾗ καὶ ᾗ ζωὴ ἡμῶν ἀνέτειλεν δι' αὐτοῦ, καὶ τοῦ θανάτου αὐτοῦ ὃν τινες ἀρνοῦνται.—*Ignat. ad Magnes.*, viii. This is according to Cureton's shorter text

† C. Plinii. Epist. x., 97, Trajano Imperatori.

of heaven, and would bar them out from admission to the Holy Communion, which was celebrated on Sundays, as is well known. Sunday, therefore, would be *the stated day.*

Justin Martyr gives a very similar account in his First Apology (A.D., 147 *circ.*), where he very fully describes the order of such an assembly, and so mentions the day on which it is held as to show that the *status dies* mentioned by Pliny was no other than the Lord's-day mentioned by John the Divine. "And on the day called *Sun-day,* all the inhabitants " (*i.e.,* all they that are Christians) of cities or villages, " having come together into one place, read the memoirs of " the Apostles, or writings of the Prophets, so far as time allows."* Now these few words are exactly descriptive of a Christianized Synagogue. When they were Jews, and no more, they read the Haphtarah, or so much of it, with an address or a conversation, as time allowed. When they became Christians in faith, but still retaining their habits as Jews, and cherishing the consciousness of being descendants of Abraham, they added to the Prophetic explanation or enforcement of the Law the more complete exposition of it afforded by the memoirs of the Apostles, or in other words the Gospels, the Acts of the Apostles, and their other writings. This feature in Justin's description is of the highest importance, for it exhibits a link of continuity in the primitive Christian practice, where the Sabbath habits of elder times were faithfully retained, and the change of day, although the celebration of peculiarly Christian worship on the Sunday, all at once introduced in the exclusively Christian congregations, was in other respects gradual, and effected without any of the inconvenience of a sudden revolution. It gives me no trouble to account for this synagogue-like manner of worship and communion, but enables me to understand the reason why the Jews did

---

* Just. Mart. Apol., i. 67.

not denounce the Christians as Sabbath-breakers, which they certainly would have done if Barnabas had not been mistaken.

Tertullian, who wrote at least half a century later than Justin, referred to the Sunday services of Christians, and notes that on the Lord's day they did not kneel in prayer, but stood up, as in the posture of confidence and joy.*

From these observations, made during a period of at least a hundred and seventy years after the Resurrection of Christ, we learn that in spite of many erroneous notions entertained by eminent members of the Church, the Lord's day was hallowed with great solemnity, and on this point there is not, I think, any conflicting evidence. Without multiplying quotations, therefore, I will now content myself with transcribing a commemorative prayer from the Apostolic Constitutions. Neither the authorship nor the date is certain, but critics agree that those constitutions were written early enough to be classed with Ante-Nicene writings, and may be confidently referred to for evidence of what was the prevailing faith and custom in that early age. Here, then, we have a Sabbath-prayer such as Christians before Constantine would use.

" O Lord Almighty, who didst create the world by Christ,
" and didst ordain the Sabbath in remembrance thereof,
" because thou wast resting from thy works, in order to our
" study of thy laws, and didst appoint the festal days for the
" delight of our souls, that we might attain to the wisdom
" which is by Thee created; as He was born for us of a
" woman, appeared in this life, showing in his baptism that
" He was both God and Man, suffered for us with thy per-
" mission, and died, and by thy power rose again. Wherefore
" also we solemnly assemble to keep the feast of the Resurrec-
" tion on the Lord's day. We rejoice for that victory over

---

* Tertul. de Orat., xxiii.

"death, bringing life and immortality to light. We rejoice that by Him thou hast brought the nations together to thyself, to be a peculiar people, the true Israel, the beloved of God, to behold God. For thou, O Lord, leddest our fathers out of the land of Egypt, and deliveredst them from the iron furnace, and from the clay, and from the making of bricks, and from the hand of Pharaoh, and from the servants of Pharaoh, and leddest them through the sea as if it were dry land, and didst nourish them in the wilderness with all manner of good things, and gavest them for law ten commandments, spoken with thine own voice, and written with thine own hand.

"Thou didst command them to keep the Sabbath, not giving a pretence for idleness, but an incitement to godliness, for the knowledge of thy might, for the avoidance of evil, even so dost thou now inclose them as within a strong fortress, that, being taught, they may exult in the sevenfold blessing. For this (thou givest them) one week and seven weeks, a seventh month and a seventh year; and of this year a seventh revolution, which is the Jubilee, the fiftieth year, the year of remission, that men may have no pretence for even seeming to be ignorant. Therefore there is every Sabbath freedom to take rest, that on the Sabbath-day no one may let an angry word escape his lips. For the Sabbath is the restingtime for all creation, the perfecting of the world, for the searching into laws, for giving praise acceptable to God in return for the things He hath given unto men.

"Above all of them is the Lord's day. This day sets before us him that is our Mediator, our Guardian, our Lawgiver; the Author of our Resurrection; the First-born of all Creation; the Word of God; the Man that was born of Mary without human Father; that lived among us without blame; that was crucified under Pontius Pilate; that died and rose up again from the dead. Therefore "this day is called the Lord's. To Thee, O Lord, let "thanksgiving be rendered for all things; for by Thee is "this grace given which, by its greatness, covers and sur-"passes all."*

The worshipping congregations that, in that age of martyrdoms for the truth's sake, could appreciate the excellence of this truly scriptural prayer, could also perceive the force of that memorable sentence, "The Son of Man is Lord also of "the Sabbath-day." The Christians of that age, thus recounting the chief events of human history, exulted in the joyous memories of the day which then, as of old, was consecrated to holy gladness, when men put off the sackcloth, and wiped away the tears. They saw humanity advancing in the path of life, led on by Jesus, Prince of Immortality, all that was good cherished and matured, and none of it cast away as out of date. The converted Pharisee, having his eyes opened, falls back from the oral to the written law, and to the imperishable history, there to learn that the Lord of the Sabbath is the same yesterday, to-day, and for ever.

With shame and sorrow we confess that throughout the greater part of nominal Christendom the perception of the origin, the nature, and the blessedness of the Sabbath has for ages faded away, except where, in personal experience, it has been revived, or the public conscience has been quickened in a nation or a province. We mourn because of a strange delusion that Christians are too spiritual to suffer what they call Sabbatarian formality, too free to brook Sabbatarian restraint. Yet such a notion is avowed by theologians of high culture, and, we would fain believe, of unquestionable sincerity. I will now endeavour to indicate the chief source, as it seems to me, of the lamentable misconception.

---

* Constitut. Apostolic., lib. vii., cap. 36.

CHAPTER XII.

EARLY DIVERSITY OF TEACHING AND CUSTOM.

CONCERNING the Lord's-day, hallowed by the Resurrection of the Saviour, there was no doubt. That day was observed by all who bore his name. But it was not so with the Sabbath. The Sacred Rest, distinctly and properly called Sabbath, and the seventh day of the week, on which men rested, were unhappily confounded, as if the *day* and the cessation from labour on the day, had but one and the same name, or as if the holiness of the rest depended on the ordinal number of the day. The simplicity and spirituality of Holy Scripture were faded from the minds of men, and in few of the chief teachers of the early Church was there a correct perception of the fundamental institutions of revealed religion. Dimness of perception was at once the cause and the effect of dulness of conscience.

Cyril of Jerusalem, for example, who wrote his catecheses some time within the first half of the fourth century, taught that Sabbaths ought to be utterly abandoned. "Flee," said he, "every diabolic action. Neither give heed to the Dragon " nor to the Apostate . . . to the predictions of astrologers, " nor to auguries, nor to omens, nor to the fabulous predic- " tions of heathens. Poisoning, incantation, raising the " spirits of the departed, let such things not be heard of." He exhorted his catechumens to abstain from all intemperance, gluttony, and voluptuousness; to be above avarice and usury; to refrain from frequenting heathen spectacles, and from using enchantments to keep away diseases. "Turn " away," said he, "from all the vile company of taverns.

"*Reject all observance of Sabbaths,* and say not of any sort "of meats which is indifferent that it is profane or unclean."* So wildly did he confound the sacred duty of Sabbath observance with pagan abominations. Because the Jews were zealous, in their mistaken way, as regarded the Sabbath, he thought that it became him to reject what they perverted, rather than restore it.

Happily, however, this was not yet a general mistake; nor could it be so long as good men read the Bible with intelligence, and distinguished what was originally of Divine appointment from the traditions of men. The old Sabbath-day and the Lord's day were for some time both observed by many Christians. On neither of those days would they fast, except on the great Sabbath, as it was called, between Good Friday and Easter day, which was kept as a fast in remembrance of our Lord's lying in the tomb.† "You must regard "the Sabbath and the Lord's day," say the Apostolic Constitutions, "as festal days, because we make remembrance "of the Creation on one, and of the Resurrection on the "other."‡ This usage was adopted in Abyssinia, and is still retained there. The foreigner may still observe that the Abyssinian will not travel on Saturday.

The Sabbath-day was chiefly remembered in the Eastern Church, where a broader and more scriptural view of the original institution prevailed, as is expressed in the comprehensively commemorative prayer quoted above from the Apostolic Constitutions.§ Athanasius speaks very clearly on the subject in his treatise on the Sabbath and Circumcision, and his homily *on the corn-field* (Matt. xii.) begins with these

---

* Cyril. Hicros, Cat. iv. 23.
† Tertul. de Jejun., xv. Ambros. de Elia et Jejun., x. Con. Apost., lxiv.
‡ Const. Apost., vii., 23. § Chapter xi. *supra.*

remarkable words: "We are met together on the Sabbath-day, not that we are affected with Judaism, for we have nothing to do with false Sabbaths, but are come together on this day that we may worship Jesus, the Lord of the Sabbath. Once, indeed, the Sabbath was honourable with these ancients, and the Lord changed the day of the Sabbath for the Lord's-day."* This statement is entirely borne out by Socrates, who says that the Egyptians of Alexandria, and they who inhabit the Thebaid, assemble in congregations on the Sabbath, but "they do not then partake of the mysteries as Christians are accustomed to do (on the Lord's day), but eat all kinds of pleasant food. They communicate after the evening has closed." The same historian, speaking of the congregations in Constantinople, says that they assemble in the churches on the Lord's day, and the *two* festal days of the week, and sing hymns responsive.†

With all this pious observance there was a certain mingling of will-worship, which gave rise to an injurious diversity, ever growing wider and wider. Constantine the Great again introduced a new element of confusion by taking the Lord's day into the list of festivals, so counting it among the Gentile feasts as if it were one of them. He gave it his imperial sanction, and the reader of his law would infer that he was rather influenced by observing how the Christians honoured it, than by a personal persuasion of the Divine appointment. Gradually he learned a little better, and some of his successors learned better still, yet Paganism tainted their legislation, and they did but impose such restrictions on certain vocations on the Lord's day as were also obligatory on heathen festivals. Valentinian the Elder exempted Christians

---

* De Semente.   † Socrat. Hist., v. 22, vi. 8.

from the interference of officers of justice on that day,* and Valentinian the Younger, when confirming that exemption, made it more ample, and expressly recognized the religious reason, declaring that such interference on that sacred day would not only be punishable, but would be treated as a sacrilege, a violation of the appointed rites of holy religion.† Theodosius confirmed this last law in the same sense,‡ but after all, the appeal to Divine authority was indistinct, until the Sabbath seemed more imperial than divine.

The beneficent spirit of Christianity found expression in these laws, notwithstanding the defect we now complain of. Honorius, for example, ordained that judges should not only be permitted but commanded to visit the prisons every Sunday, see the prisoners, and ascertain whether the warders had refused them any of those acts of humanity which the laws allowed. He also commanded food to be distributed among the starving poor on Sundays. Persons condemned to close imprisonment were to be brought out, taken to the baths under careful custody, and brought back to the cells clean. Judges or other officers who neglected these duties on the day sanctified by Christ to deeds of mercy were to be heavily fined.§ Works of real necessity for public safety or preservation of life were always to be done on the Christian Sabbath. This kind of legislation continued for some ages, and in various countries of Christendom, but was not always characterized with equal wisdom, nor enforced with equal honesty.

While piety retained its vigour good customs lasted, and true followers of Christ hallowed his day with solemn assemblage in spite of almost every difficulty. When watched

---

* Cod. Theodos., lib. viii. Tit. viii., lex 1.
† Tit. viii., lex 3.   ‡ Lib. ii. Tit. viii., lex 2.
§ Cod. Theodos., lib. ix. Tit. xii., lex 7.

by heathen persecutors, who dragged away those whom they detected in acts of Christian worship, and delivered them to magistrates who offered them the choice between apostasy or martyrdom, they prepared themselves for death, assembling at night, and concluding their devotions before the dawn of day.

Tertullian advised his brethren to do thus. "Every day," said he, " we are beset, every day we are betrayed, and very " often attacked in the midst of our companies and congrega-" tions." But he would not have them shun the danger by neglecting the duty, nor avert it by bribing the officers of pagan justice. The *faith* that could remove a mountain could also remove a soldier. Innocence, not concealment, would save them from false accusers. It was best and safest that they should hallow the Lord's-day as the Lord himself had hallowed it, with the word of God, prayer, and communion.*

Christians refrained from attending pagan spectacles on that day, and after a time the law assisted them in such abstention. If the day for public entertainments—the emperor's birthday, for example—fell on a Sunday, the celebration was deferred until Sunday was past, that Christian worshippers might not be disturbed in their congregations or their homes.

Yet there was a darker side. Folly and superstition persisted in their course. The meanest forms of Rabbanism crept in, to debase the earnest but untaught zeal of Jewish converts. Origen makes mention of certain heretics who taught that the law of Moses required men to sit still in their houses on the Sabbath, and not move out of their seats. Every person, they insisted, should maintain the same posture the whole day through until sunset. To mitigate this absurd

---

* Tertullian, Apologia vii. De Fugâ xiv.

severity, some undertook to moderate the alleged severity of God's law by help of convenient traditions, and an enlargement of the meaning of sentences which that law, after all, did not contain. The importation of those trifles into the Christian Church provoked idle controversies, and tended to bring Sabbath-keeping into contempt. Fanatic zeal wrestled with godless opposition; but, amidst consequent confusion, traces may be found of the soundest principle, and efforts were made by the Church from time to time to lead her members into a course of moderate and scriptural observance. So the Council of Laodicea recorded its judgment that "Chris-"tians ought not to Judaize and be idle on the Sabbath-day, " but should work for themselves on that day, preferring to "rest on the Lord's day, if they can, as Christians. But "if they are found idle, let them be anathema from Christ."* The expression, *if they can,* εἰ δύναιντο, may hint at works of real necessity or mercy, or it may hint at an expedient compromise. Here we find extreme rigour on one side and indefinite exception on the other, and time has too abundantly shown the evil consequences of such compromise and contradiction.

---

* Conc. Laodic. Can. xxix.

CHAPTER XIII.

ROMISH PERVERSION OF THE FOURTH COMMANDMENT.

The diversity of teaching and practice which began in the earlier ages of Christianity, and spread rapidly thenceforth, is alone sufficient to account for the depravation of doctrine in regard to the Christian Sabbath which is prevalent at the present time. The causes of diversity have been indicated. We now come to its effects.

The Reformation of the Sixteenth Century brought to light the deplorable fact that the pretended authority of the so-called Catholic Church had superseded the one authority whereon alone the true Church of Christ depends for its existence. That I may not seem to exaggerate, I will confine myself as closely as possible to what I find written in the Roman Catechism, a summary of doctrine prepared by order of the Pope Saint Pius V. for the guidance of Parish Priests in their ministrations to the people, and universally used for this purpose, under papal sanction, at the present day.*

The Fourth Commandment of the Decalogue, counted *third* in the Roman Church, is quoted literally, and so far accepted by the highest authority in that Church. The Catechism teaches to the following effect :—

1. That this Commandment of the Law prescribes the external worship† which we owe to God. It follows naturally from the First Commandment, for we cannot but venerate

---

* Catechismus ad Parochos. Pars. iii., cap. 4.

† *External worship* is not mentioned at all in this commandment. It may be implied, as much more also is implied, but certainly it is not *prescribed*.

with external act Him whom we inwardly adore. And as this cannot easily be done by those who are immersed in worldly business, a certain time was appointed when such acts may be conveniently performed.

2. That as this Commandment is of the kind to produce wonderfully good effects, it is very important that the Priest should explain it well. The first word, *Remember*, should move him to the greater diligence. He should remind the faithful that they are to remember it, and to that end frequently admonish and instruct them. The faithful observance of this commandment will help them to keep all the others. It will help them, because the more careful they are to go to Church on " Feast-days"* to hear the Word of God, and be instructed in His laws, the more heartily will they keep them all. References are made to many passages in the Old Testament, from Genesis to Ezekiel.

3. Princes and magistrates have to be admonished and exhorted that, in all that concerns the worship of God, they help with their authority the prelates of the Church, and command the people to obey the precepts of the priests. They must teach the people in what respects this commandment *agrees* with the others, and how it *differs* from them. " For by this means they will know why we do not observe " the Sabbath, but the Lord's day, and keep that holy." †

---

* *On Feast-days*, with which Sundays are studiously and systematically confounded. It is notorious that in many of the common School Catechisms in use on the Continent, the Ten Commandments are not printed in full, but only in summary. The Fourth or *Third* Commandment is reduced to a very brief sentence—" Keep the Feasts."

† This confounds the institution with the day, and the confusion is wilful. Again let us insist that the Sabbath is not set aside, but retained, and that, under the example and authority of our Lord Jesus Christ, its observance is transferred from the seventh day of the week to the first.

4. That the difference of this commandment from the others is clear, for, unlike this, the other precepts of the decalogue are natural, perpetual, and cannot vary. Hence it follows that, although the Law of Moses is abrogated, the Christian people still keep the commandments that are in the two tables. Not because Moses commanded, but because they are in agreement with Nature, by force of which men are impelled to keep them.* But this command to keep the Sabbath, if we consider the time appointed, is not fixed and constant, but may be changed.† It (the commandment) is not moral, but ceremonial, for we are neither taught nor led by Nature to worship God on that day more than on any other, but the people of Israel began to keep the Sabbath-day from the time when they were set free from slavery under Pharaoh.‡

5. On the death of Christ, when the other Hebrew observances and ceremonies became obsolete, the observance of the Sabbath also was to be taken away. It passed away with all the other shadows. With reference to it the Apostle wrote to the Galatians, "Ye observe days and months, and "times and years. I am afraid of you, that I have bestowed

---

* Such a force of Nature, compelling men to keep God's commandments, is unknown in fact, and the notion of it is contrary to Holy Scripture, and to the witness of our own conscience. Nature does not impel men to abstain from fornication nor to tell the truth, but Nature when unrestrained, impels them to every variety of sin. "To be "carnally minded is death."

† "*May be changed.*" It is easy to affirm that the day is optional, but not so to prove that it is. We have not known any more than one such change, and that one was attended by circumstances of inconceivable solemnity, and accomplished under the immediate guidance of our Lord himself, who is Lord of the Sabbath.

‡ Whenever the people of Israel began to keep Sabbaths, it is certain that the progenitors of all mankind began on the first clear day of time, in Paradise. We see that the law is not ceremonial but moral.

" upon you labour in vain." He writes the same to the Colossians.*

6. But this commandment agrees not with the others in any rite or ceremony, except in so far as it has anything in it which pertains to manners and the law of Nature. For the worship of God, and religion which is expressed in this commandment, corresponds with that in Nature which prompts us to employ a few hours in matters relating to the worship of God †. The heathens do this, and it is natural in man to devote some time to eating and drinking, to rest, to sleep, and such like.

7. "For this reason the apostles determined to consecrate "to divine worship that one day of the seven which is first, "and which they called the Lord's day." And then the catechism has references to passages which we have quoted from the Apocalypse, and the first epistle to the Corinthians.

But here is a very bold perversion of the truth. It was not the Apostles who *determined* to consecrate the first day of the week to divine worship. They did not determine to meet the Lord on their way to Emmaus. They did not determine that He should appear to them suddenly when they were in Jerusalem, any more than they determined that He should rise on that day from the dead. They did not determine that He should meet them and converse with them again on that

---

* This cannot be proved to refer to the Sabbath, any more than it could be proved to belong to the modern Roman kalendar, or to the Papal jubilees. As for the Sabbath being part of the Mosaic ceremonial, that is historically untrue, as I believe I have clearly shown.

† To worship God, then, is to the Roman theologians as natural as to eat and drink. To eat and drink as religious as to worship God. The Pagan and the Papal Roman, therefore, may well agree in pronouncing the elephant to be *animal religiosior*, because he lifts up his trunk towards heaven when he drinks.

day week. They did not determine that the Holy Ghost should descend on them again on the day of Pentecost, nor that the stupendous event that followed should take place on that day. If the Apostles had determined on so grave a measure as that of keeping Sabbath apart from the synagogue, and consecrating another day instead of the seventh to the solemn worship of God, they would surely have conferred, and prayed, and perhaps also fasted. At mention of so great a charge some sincere zealot for the Law would have raised an objection. On this important point, as on that of circumcision, there would inevitably have been some debate, and probably a difficulty in deciding, to be settled after all by lot. The decision accomplished, a public notification also would have been indispensable.

If the Apostles had assumed the responsibility of deciding for so formal a secession from the whole body of their nation, they would have held themselves ready to assign a reason, and prepared to rebut the charge of altering the Sabbath—a charge which the Jews make now, but was not heard of then. The Apostles, it is certain, were not charged with Sabbath-breaking, for they greatly reverenced the Sabbath. They did not absent themselves from the synagogue worship until, in city after city, united worship became impossible. Then at length, when the assemblage of Christians on the Lord's-day, and their separation or expulsion from the synagogues on the seventh day, became general, there was no need of Apostolic agreement, nor was any such agreement, so far as I can remember to have read, appealed to in justification of the change. Quite sufficient was the unspeakably stronger reason that Christ himself had led the way, and that wondrously mighty workings of the Holy Ghost had confirmed the Christian Sabbath-day so firmly that it could not be set aside.

All that we can say is that, in this figment of an apostolic institution, independent of any directly Divine sanction or command, the thread of history is lost; that in counting amongst Mosaic ceremonies a Divine appointment made at the Creation, they are guilty of a flagrant contempt of history, and an equally manifest contempt of the supreme authority of the Divine Legislator—an error as palpable as it is self-refuting,

The assertions of the Roman Catechism are in full accordance with the notions current in that Church and in some Protestant Churches, but utterly at variance with the authentic records of the New Testament and the venerable muniments of primeval antiquity which are treasured in the Old. We must therefore dismiss all such gratuitous inventions from our thoughts when we seek to arrive at any sure conclusion in regard to God's holy Sabbath.

The Canonists, however, are perfectly agreed in slighting all scriptural authority. By them the Lord's-day is counted with holidays, and is chiefly treated of in the title *De feriis*. A council in France ordains that *all Dominical days* (which may or may not be Sundays) be observed with perfect veneration, with abstinence from all unlawful work, from marketing, impleading in courts, passing sentences of imprisonment or death, and administering oaths. A Pope, Alexander III., coolly determines that, "Although the page, both of the Old
" and the New Testament, has given the seventh day, espe-
" cially, for human rest, and the Church has decreed that *as*
" *well that day as* the birthdays of holy martyrs are to be ob-
" served, and on them all servile work is to be set aside, we
" indulge that it be lawful to your parishioners, both on Sun-
" days and on other feasts, except on the greater solemnities
" of the year, if herrings come near the shore, the necessity
" for taking them being urgent, it may be done, provided that
" a suitable portion of the catch, when it is made, be given to

"the neighbouring churches, and to Christ's poor"—that is to say, the monks! Pius V. advances yet beyond his predecessors, by expressly confounding Sundays with common holidays, when he commands that "all Dominical days"—*dies Dominici* having been hitherto the name of Sundays only—" and espe-
" cially those which are kept as holidays, *feriati*, in honour of
" God, the blessed Virgin Mary, or the Holy Apostles, be
" observed with all veneration; that on such days all persons
" frequent the churches, pay devout attention to the Divine
" offices, abstain from all unlawful and servile work, make no
" marketings, transact no profane business, and have no noisy
" litigations."* Thus does the Pope for the time being pretend to be Lord of the Sabbath, and reduce it to a common holiday.

When the Popes had their acknowledged representatives in this country, and our kings were sometimes trodden under foot by them, they maintained the same pretension to be the fountains of all spiritual authority, alike supreme over the laws of England and the Word of God. Traces of this contempt of God's law are to this day too distinct; and although the archiepiscopal constitutions issued before the Reformation have not now any legal force, they are so far acknowledged as to have considerable moral influence. As old documents, at least, they convey much instruction, and a canonical exposition of the Ten Commandments by Archbishop Peckham in the thirteenth century tells us how much the Christian Sabbath had been lowered after the establishment of Papal power. The words are these:—

" When it is said in the Third Commandment, Remember
" that thou keep holy the Sabbath day, that Christian religious
" worship is prescribed to which clergymen and laymen are

---

* Decret. Greg., lib. i. Tit. xi., cap. 1.; lib. ii. Tit. ix., cap. 2, 3. Septim. Decret., lib. iii. Tit. ix., cap. 2.

" equally bound. There, however, it must be known that the
" obligation to keep holiday on the legal Sabbath according
" to the form of the Old Testament altogether expired, like
" other ceremonies, with the law. And under the New Testa-
" ment, the present manner of setting ourselves at liberty for
" Divine service on Sundays and the other solemn days which
" are set apart for this by authority of the Church is sufficient.
" On those days the manner of resting from labour is not to
" be taken from Jewish superstition, but from canonical
" institutes." * When Peckham wrote this constitution Wycliffe was not born, and the Bible was so nearly unknown in England that he could venture, without fear of scandal, to call that law which the Most High God wrote on the tables of stone by the contemptuous epithet of Jewish superstition. When Lyndewode garnished the text of his provincial with learned notes, the remains of Wycliffe had been but lately exhumed and burnt at Lutterworth, and Englishmen in general were not yet sufficiently enlightened to perceive the imposture which would set the damning brand of superstition and hated Judaism upon the pure and holy law of God which our Incarnate Lord magnified and made honourable, and to which He joyfully submitted himself, that He might leave us an example to walk in his steps. Submission to this law as it is written in the Book of Exodus, and in many other parts of the Old Testament, is not a ceremony in any correct sense whatever. Obedience to parents or paying one's debts might with as great propriety be called a ceremony.

---

* Lyndewode Provinciale de officio Archipresbyteri.

CHAPTER XIV.

OLD ENGLISH LAW.

The whole truth as to the original, universal, and unchanging Sabbath—the truth which had lingered long among the Fathers of the earlier Church—was now cast aside, yet it is doubtful whether a traditional remembrance of it was quite eradicated from the heart of England. We look back into our national history, and see most clearly that in the Anglo-Saxon times it was not possible for papal arrogance to frown down the cherished convictions of our forefathers, or to abolish the salutary customs which, long before the Monk Augustine sighted the Kentish cliffs, our fathers had learned from their teachers and from the written Word of God.

One cannot read many pages of Bede's Ecclesiastical History of England without perceiving that, when the venerable historian wrote, the Holy Bible was read familiarly by both the preachers and their congregations. He relates explicitly that the sacred books were read, in his time, by the Angles, Britons, Scots, Picts, and Latins, by each in his own language.*

A glance at our laws will show that Sabbath-observance prevailed in England, together with a solemn recognition of the authority of Holy Scripture; and, on reflection, the student perceives that in this respect our country had the advantage over every other European State during eight centuries at least before the Reformation. The numerous documents collected by Spelman indicate great activity at Rome, and in England also, on the part of Roman emissaries. Truly national

---

* Hist. Eccles., lib. i.

religious life among the Anglo-Saxons must be traced to a higher source, and may in great part be attributed to Christian influence flowing through Roman and British channels in very early times. Canons abound, indeed, of very doubtful authenticity, dated back in the sixth and seventh centuries, conceived in a strongly ecclesiastical spirit, and bearing marks of much later hands, but these I leave with the single observation that they cast no sure light on the subject before us.

We may begin, however, with Ine, or Ina, King of the West Saxons, perhaps the first Anglo-Saxon king who issued laws framed with a royal care for the advancement of religion among his subjects, to be supported by his own authority. The code of Ina, said to have been promulgated about the year 693, contains a law *on Sunday work*, worded thus: " If a bondman works on Sunday by his lord's command, let " him be free, and let the lord pay thirty-shillings for a fine. " But if the servant works without his knowledge, let his hide " pay for it, or the price of his hide. But if the free servant " works on that day without his lord's command, let him pay " for it with his freedom, or sixty shillings. And if a priest " does it, let him be twice guilty."*

Be it observed that in the laws of Ina there is no mention of any other day so guarded against desecration by labour, but only the Sunday. Such mention there certainly would have been if the Bishops and Eldermen had so advised; but it is evident that Sunday was not yet counted as a mere church-feast in our country.

At the Council of Berkhamstead, in the fifth year of Withred, King of Kent, held under Bertwald, Archbishop of Canterbury, the following canons were recorded under the title of *Judgments of Withred:* " If a servant, by his master's

---

* Spelmani Concilia., An. Chr. 693. Mœ. 3.

"orders, does any servile work on Sunday eve, after sun-set, "or before Monday eve, when the sun has gone down, let the "master pay eighty shillings." "If a servant takes to the "road on that day, let him pay six shillings to his master, or "his hide for it."*

Such were the first rude Saxon laws, severe and summary, quite in character with the people and the age. All those laws were of the same character, and worthy of commendation for their simplicity, at least; but soon the simplicity diminished, the rude chieftain figured less conspicuously, the priest more, and an ecclesiastical aim became increasingly apparent. But when good King Alfred assumed the sovereignty of united England, he did not leave inferior persons to draft his laws, but gave to the work of legislation the fully concentrated energies of his own heart and mind. Unlike young King Ina, who sheltered himself behind the injunction of his father and the advice of his bishops, Alfred cast off all such trammels, and in proceeding to reduce the fruit of long study into a written form, he wrote the Ten Commandments first, which, by the way, he would not have done if he had considered them to be part of the law of Moses, made for his people only. For giving this Divine summary of all primary duties to God and man the chief place in a national code, I am not aware that Alfred had any precedent, but he thereby signified that he laid his crown at the feet of the King of Kings, and led the way in an avowed subjection of the laws of England to the law of God. The first sentence of his code was this: "The "Lord spake to Moses these words." After the first commandment followed the third, and one might at first sight imagine that the second was omitted by the scribes in copying; but that conjecture is not confirmed by what follows, for

---

* Ibid., An. 697.

after the nine have been transcribed in full, the omission of the second is tacitly acknowledged by subjoining in immediate continuation the words: "Make not to thyself golden gods, nor silvern." The fact was that the second Council of Nicea had sanctioned image-worship in open contradiction to the erased commandment; and it is probable that the practice of omitting it from the Decalogue when taken from the Bible to be read, or given to the people in a separate form, had become established, and that King Alfred, although he followed that example, made the rejected commandment doubly conspicuous, first by the marked omission, and then by setting against the priestly mutilation of God's law his own implied protest by that sentence written at the foot. The English people, therefore, could not make for themselves gods of gold or silver without express contempt of human authority as well as Divine.

At considerable length the first King of England borrowed sentence from Holy Scripture, or he wrote down their substances in his own language; and if any one wishes to understand his reason for this peculiar treatment of the Decalogue, he has only to ponder the few lines following: "I King "Alfred have collected these sanctions into one, and put them "all into writing. Our elders did certainly observe a good "part of them; much also appeared to me worthy to be "religiously observed by ourselves in the present age; some, "however, which seemed less proper for us, I have "purposely omitted, partly after taking counsel of wise men, "and some, partly on reflection of my own, *I have restored*." * Many things enacted by Ina, Offa, and Ethelbert, he had advisedly omitted.

Subsequently, in his compact with Guthrun the Dane,

---

* Ibid., An. 887.

Alfred repeated, in substance, the law of Ina forbidding work, traffic, and legal or judicial proceedings on Sunday. It was indeed necessary for the common peace that the Danes should adapt themselves to the customs of the English, and respect their conscience, for the Sunday was, in full reality, a day of rest and piety. Biographers and homilists agree in their descriptions of the habits of good men, and the customs of the English people in general, making it evident that on that holy day earnest preachers were surrounded by congregations of attentive hearers, who crowded the churches, not for mass, but for prayers and sermon. They pressed to hear the Word of God, and in their houses they gave hospitable entertainment to the strangers who came from far to unite in those sacred exercises.*

Laws to the same effect were in force through all the Saxon period, as may be seen in Spelman, Wheloc's Bede, and other authorities; but with the Norman Conquest, Sabbath-keeping properly so called ceased to be under legal sanction. This change in the law of England certainly did not arise from any hesitation to enforce religious duties by the secular power, for on that point the rulers of England felt no delicacy. Neither was the care now abandoned by the civil magistrate taken on himself by the priest. Sundays were now to be accounted as holidays appointed by the Church; custom sufficed to keep up those holidays, and they were kept clear of everything like what is called Puritanical restraint. Theologians, such as they were, coldly acknowledged the Divine appointment of a Sabbath before Christ, but they classed it with Levitical ceremonies, and taught that it had been ordained by Moses for temporary reasons, but was, as a Mosaic ceremony, set aside by Christ. So Englishmen were

---

* Wheloc's Bede, pp. 240—244.

taught before the Reformation, and so, in spite of the Reformation, many continue still to teach. To the present day an erroneous notion that the religious observance of Sunday becomes obligatory by the mere force of ecclesiastical or even civil authority vitiates our English law, and the impression that the obligation is laid on us by canon law and Act of Parliament vitiates the public conscience. As for canon law, although every Church must have its own regulations, they are only binding on its members so long as they continue in communion, and even on them are only binding so long as it is not found necessary to alter them, but when the law of God is reduced to the same level, it has already suffered a criminal contempt, and He who gave it surely vindicates his own honour, sooner or later. The Divine law may not be treated as if it were an Act of Parliament.

Now, although King Alfred and his Saxon predecessors may seem to have exposed the Fourth Commandment to this dishonour, it has to be remembered that they did not pretend to enact the Sabbath law, but to enforce its observance under penalty in case of disobedience; that the original commandment, as it was laid down by that illustrious king, had its full weight, and that its due observance became habitual; and the sanctities of the day so deeply impressed the English mind as to create a tradition which has outlived every adverse influence. *The English Sunday* still distinguishes our country from most others, while yet the defective teaching of some, and the hostile efforts of others, who seek to set aside Sabbath-keeping altogether, should induce Christian people to study the subject for themselves, and to study it at the fountain-head of all reliable information, namely, the written Word of God.

CHAPTER XV.

AFTER THE REFORMATION, ON THE CONTINENT AND IN ENGLAND.

CHURCHMEN before the Reformation, in all parts of Europe, were perforce agreed in keeping to the externals of the prescribed religion, but the latent persuasion of men's minds was various. In England, where scriptural Christianity had early preoccupied the ground, a respect for the Lord's day lingered in the recesses of society, at least where a wealthy and political clergy had not utterly overpowered the force of public conscience with sacerdotal pride and luxury. From whatever cause it may have been, the Protestant Reformation found the English and Scottish populations very differently affected from the German and the Swiss.

The position taken by Luther cannot be sufficiently deplored. Involved, as he was, in perpetual controversy, and absorbed in such studies and occupations as were forced on him by the exigencies of each passing moment, every topic was in some degree neglected which did not directly concern, or seem to concern, the great quarrel with the Papacy. That great but impetuous Reformer took many things for granted to the last, and, as a court preacher, was no doubt in entire agreement with his audience when, so early as the year 1544, he took upon himself to descant on the present subject. The occasion of his sermon was the consecration of a chapel at Torgau, in Saxony, the first place of worship newly-erected in that electorate after the state became Protestant. Having been requested to preach, and not being willing, like many modern preachers, to give an insignificant string of commonplaces on a special occasion, he thought it right to deliver his judgment on some matters relating to Divine worship. That occasion, indeed, was extraordinary. Under the sanction of the Elector, all the rites accustomed for the consecration of churches were laid aside, and it was deemed sufficient for consecration of the new building to offer prayer, with reading and exposition of Holy Scripture.

Luther selected for his portion the passage in the Gospel (Luke xiv. 2) where our Lord discourses on the lawfulness of healing the sick on the Sabbath-day. A conscientious exposition of the passage would have been abundantly sufficient to provide suitable instruction for his hearers, and reproof also for the sacerdotal Pharisees, whom it was his constant duty to unmask; but he went further. The Sabbath, he said, was the seventh day, anciently appointed for Divine worship to the Jews, palpably forgetting, what he certainly knew, that the Sabbath was not given to the Jews, nor yet to Moses and the Hebrews, nor yet even to Abraham, but to Adam and to the whole world with him. Harping rudely on the slackened chord, he told them that the Church had liberty to change the Sabbath from Saturday to Sunday, not doubting that such a change might be made on a grave reason occurring, *by the power and consent of Christians,* although not at the pleasure of individuals. But the man who was accustomed to bring the most exact reasoning to bear upon the most explicit evidence, content with nothing less, when his object was to establish a cardinal truth or to overthrow some colossal error, brought no evidence at all to show that any such agreement had ever taken place, but treated that matter as if it were not of consequence enough to be debated; nor did he seem to think that, in the change of day actually made, any Divine authority had intervened. He pronounced, however, that when the Lord's day was so instituted by the change from the seventh day to the first, no change should be made again without sufficient reason, and *advised*, therefore, that the Lord's-day should be retained as formerly, *saving Christian liberty!* A salvo this, which might have left Christendom divided into as many parts as there are days in the week, saving every man's liberty, and overlooking the two decisive facts which must ever forbid a further change by any human authority, namely, the Resurrection of our Lord on the first day of the week, which Christians now commemorate, and the actual consecration of the day by the Saviour himself and all his apostles and disciples, as recorded in the New Testament. The first of these facts gives the reason for the change; the second conveys the warrant for its accomplishment. In that unhappy moment Luther forgot them both.

Jewish superstition, of which, however, an exceedingly minute proportion yet remained either in Germany or the Papal States, was to be rejected. Pious Sabbath-worship—the fervent reformer instructed his hearers—consisted in preaching the Word of God and getting it impressed upon the mind, and also offering prayer to God in the congregation with greater fervour and effect.* Now if this were all—if the Christian Sabbath-day were not actually sanctioned by our Lord and his inspired servants for the perpetuation of the holy institution which He had always honoured, and of which He was the Lord, but was only accepted by consent of Christians, with a salvo for their Christian liberty if it befel them to change their mind, then it would have no authoritative sanction. In that case it would be what Luther made it, and what it still is practically made in Germany, nothing more than a well-intended human institution, placed at the mercy of a human weakness, foolishly and falsely called Christian liberty.

---

* Seckendorfii Hist. Lutherana, lib. iii., sect. 30, cxviii.

The indisputable facts of sacred history which others have collected before me, and which I have again sought for myself in Holy Scripture, and set before the reader, is evidence clear enough to show that the general observance of the Sabbath on the first day of the week was not appointed *by* the Church, but was ordered *for* the Church and for the world by our Lord himself, and then again and again confirmed by himself with many stupendous signs and most precious blessings to his obedient disciples.

Luther failed more sadly. It has been too truly said that he advised his congregation to dance, and sing, and make themselves merry on Sundays, because the Sunday was given them for their enjoyment. I remember to have read a passage to this effect in his German works, and made note of it at the time, but cannot now lay hand on the note, so as to produce the passage literally; but there it is. The levity of the eminent reformer, following the levity of canonists and monkish preachers, was effectually communicated to the Lutheran Church in Germany, and has now become inveterate.

Melancthon, worthily distinguished as the theologian of the German Reformation, was equally at fault. He made light of the *Dies Dominicus* of Romanism; he mysticised the Sabbath of the Old Testament, chiefly mentioning it as a figure of rest from sin and trouble in this world, or of rest in heaven. The practical benefit of a real Sabbath-day he does not seem to have clearly comprehended.*

---

* A Lutheran Sunday is notoriously godless, and of the two it is perhaps worse than a Sunday in Rome. Worse, because in Rome there is no pretence of Reformation, nor boast of scriptural religion, but in Berlin there is sometimes a high pretension to personal piety, combined with an utter disregard of the first command of God, and a shameless persistence in the sin of open Sabbath-breaking, which has ever been visited with signal marks of God's displeasure. Hence the Lutheran pulpit is

Zuinglius was poisoned at the same fountain. In his annotations on the Gospel according to St. Matthew, he professes to learn from the narrative of plucking the ears of corn on the Sabbath-day, that Sabbath-keeping was a part of Jewish bondage from which our Saviour set his disciples free, and he endeavours to comfort his readers with the reflection that " when Christ was made Son of Man for us," He became Lord of the Sabbath, and constituted us also lords of the Sabbath. That when Christ is ours, all that Christ has is ours also. That as He is the Head and we the members of a mystic body, we share with him in all good things. Here, he tells us, Christ does not excuse himself, but his disciples; by which we may learn that when Christ excuses all his disciples in himself, He makes them all, in himself, lords of the Sabbath. This is the unsearchable treasure of Divine goodness, that God accepts us all in his Son. For we, too, are sons of God. He is by nature the Son of God, and eternal; we are sons by adoption. Therefore, whatever is lawful for Christ, is lawful for us.

Sparing all criticism on the theology or the logic of this morsel of Helvetian divinity, I only give it as a specimen of random treatment of a most important passage of sacred history, and observe that, so far as I can find in a somewhat

---

so generally fruitless of instruction, and the population abandoned to ignorance and characterized by coarse profanity. A church, called Protestant, has been suffered to exist in the north of Europe without a Sabbath for three centuries and a half. In all that time of Sundays without Sabbath, its theologians have lost their creed, and, with a few bright exceptions—and comparatively but few—its people have yet to be awakened to a perception of the very first principles of Gospel truth and sentiment. As in the Papal kingdoms, so in Protestant Germany, the popular catechism has a false Decalogue, with the Second Commandment blotted out, and instead of the Fourth, there is only " Keep the holidays," which is just as Luther himself wrote it.

careful search, his writings do not afford a passage more distinct as regards the proper subject of the Gospel narrative; and the inevitable conviction is that to Zuinglius, as well as to Melancthon and Luther, the Sabbath served only as the Tabernacle, or the High Priest's Garments, or the Manna—just a convenient object to enrich the store of metaphor, but not to have any direct application to the life of man.

With such feeble beginnings, the leaders of the Reformation could not do much to promote obedience to the law of God embodied in the Fourth Commandment, which they were not careful to understand; and when we pause to consider how far this observance has advanced in some of the important sections of Reformed Christendom, not so much under the patronage of kings, or the inculcation of eminent divines, as from the ever-present instruction of the Bible silently speaking from its own pages, and the favouring influences of the sovereign providence of Almighty God, who still sends his blessing upon all that keep his commandments, we cannot but see that the right use of the day would be alone sufficient to justify its universal sanctification. Every church wherein a truly devout and earnest congregation is assembled brings together many families into the focus of Sabbath blessings. The soul that on this day dwells in peace, drinks in sacred knowledge, and delights in Christian communion, with retreat from the turmoil of the working days, surely shrinks from whatever desecrates the day. Not only persuaded by dint of argument, but drawn by the all-persuasive powers of God's presence and blessing, the Christian people, of whatever name, are constituted a host of defence against those who would intrench upon the barrier of separation which on this day marks off the Church of the Living God from the mere worldly territory. So far is our Sabbath from being Jewish or Patriarchal—so far is it from being legal or priestly—that it brings us nearer to heaven without conveying to our perception the sense of anything peculiar or temporary. For tranquil joy, for untainted purity, for high and inviolable privilege, it brings thoughts of Paradise, and while carrying us back into a time older than sin in this world, it gives us the taste of joys that cannot be fully realized until we enter into the eternal rest that remaineth for the people of God.

Whenever religion revives, the Sabbath revives with it. That was exemplified in France, when the Reformed Church was purified by long trial, and, being made less worldly, became more jealous for the sanctification of the Lord's-day than she had been before. In her very last general synod* she poured forth an impassioned lamentation over those unfaithful members who employed the day in worldly business, sports, and pastimes, forsaking the house of God, and giving themselves to sports and recreations, estranging their hearts from the affections and worship of God, "and from "that devotion which we are most especially obliged to upon "these holy Sabbaths of Christ's own institution."

In our own country, when religion revived in the latter part of the sixteenth century, and earnest piety was driven into nonconformity, a diligent pen sketched, in clear and strong lines, a picture of the Christian Sabbath, as it had not hitherto been seen, and infused such a new spirit into the population of England, that the sanctification of the day began in earnest, and the epithet of *Sabbatarian*, uttered by some in scorn, came to be a title of honour in the esteem of many. From that time spiritual religion sprang up again in this land, and we have now experience enough within our own borders to assure us that the morals, the happiness, and the

---

* The Synod of Loudun, 1659—60. See Quick's Sydinocon, ii. 551.

reputation of England, rise or fall as God's holy day is used for his honour, or as it is desecrated for our own indulgence.

It was far on in the reign of Queen Elizabeth that Doctor Nicholas Bownd described the wretched state of religion in this country. The ministers of religion were unprofitable. Many of them could not so much as read distinctly so as to be understood. Many could but read; to preach lay far beyond their power. Many that could preach had better have held their tongue, for they could not divide the Word of God aright. The congregations, too, were so disorderly that the voices of the people were oftentimes louder than the voice of the minister, and the church became the scene of boisterous confusion, even in the time of worship. If so the church on Sundays, what must have been the town?

In the year 1595, Dr. Bownd published a book on " The " True Doctrine of the Sabbath, held and practised of the " Church of God, both before and under the Law, and in the " time of the Gospel." In these days of rigid criticism the book would be censured as verbose and confused, and not without reason. The title, so far as I copy it, is clear enough, but the book is not so clear, because its contents are not well arranged. He does not insist with sufficient distinctness on his own proposition that the Sabbath was ordained at the Creation, but attributes its preservation, if indeed it was preserved, rather to tradition than to any known law. He begins his " doctrine " too late—in the wilderness of Arabia rather than in Paradise. Anxious, as he was, to reform the manners of England, he insisted with too great minuteness on certain particulars of duty, and so laid his work open to the criticism of the adverse party like a broad target that every shot might strike.*

---

* Sabbathum Veteris et Novi Testamenti. London, 1606. *Second Edition.*

Notwithstanding these imperfections, his book wrought wonders. It was new. Readers were not so impatient in those days as in these. The teaching was for the most part sound, and the author insisted on the authority of Holy Scripture. The clergy raised a loud outcry against Dr. Bownd, as if he wanted to make it appear that the Church had put its own festivals in the place of the weekly Sabbath, and was, therefore, an enemy of the Church. But the public voice pronounced in favour of the book, and an amazing change took place all over England, which put the priests to silence. The truth is that the reverential spirit of old England was revived, and the days of Alfred and of Bede seemed for a time to have come back again. But the public mind was not yet clear. Other less enlightened writers undertook to make it clearer.

About the year 1618, in the reign of James I., one John Thraske essayed to advance beyond Bownd by teaching that the Lord's-day was to be observed in a Jewish manner, and that Christians ought to be guided by the law of Moses in regard to clean and unclean meats. Many followed him, but he was censured in the Star Chamber, and recanted his opinions, which, however, gave a tinge of what is called Sabbatarianism to the opinions of many. After Thraske, Theophilus Bradborn, a minister in Suffolk, wrote another book more hurtful still. His doctrine was that the Mosaic Sabbath remained unchanged on the seventh day, and that " the Lord's-day is an ordinary working day, it being will-" worship and superstition to make it a Sabbath by virtue of " the Fourth Commandment." This was in 1628. In 1633, Francis White, Bishop of Ely, was appointed by Charles I. to confute Bradborn, but this bishop represented the king too well, and ran into the opposite stream of godlessness.

Puritanism and the Book of Sports now denote the two

extremes in a controversy that had better not be revived, and therefore I check my pen. The chief sources of error I have pointed out in the preceding chapters, and here we mark the beginning of an unprofitable strife. We have not now to study the doctrine of the Rabbanites, or the Fathers, or the Popes, or the Sabbatarians, but with a candid and prayerful spirit search the Scriptures, thankfully receive the Holy Sabbath as an imperishable gift of God, and use it for him. *How* to use it, the Bible and the spirit of the Bible will surely teach. The Fourth Commandment, which I have endeavoured to explain, and to show that it is a part of God's covenant with his people quite distinct from the ceremonial and civil code of Moses—this Fourth Commandment, notwithstanding its verbal adaptation, in some part, to the circumstances of the Hebrews, contains the pure Sabbatic precept, which, substantially unchanged, is the universal and perpetual law. The more of the spirit of truth we have, the more earnestly and the better we shall keep it.

CHAPTER XVI.

ON THE RIGHT OBSERVANCE OF GOD'S LAW.

If I have not utterly mistaken the spirit of the original Sabbath-law, or failed to show that it has not suffered any change from the time when it was first given to mankind until the close of the New Testament Scriptures, I have succeeded in proving that, like all other Divine ordinances, it is a law of perfect benevolence. As for human laws on the same subject, by whomsoever enacted, they are as remarkable for defect or error as the law I have been endeavouring to review is admirable for its perfection. A Constantine or a Justinian, an Alfred or a Charles, may have intended well when endeavouring to enforce God's law by statutes of their own; and I, for one, believe it to be the duty of legislators to provide for the public observance of an institution so eminently social as is this. In every state that can reasonably hope for prosperity, or expect permanence, there must be statutes to protect marriage—statutes, I am convinced, very far indeed superior to the present law of England, although the moral obligations which the law of a Christian should recognize and guard rest entirely on the primeval institution of God in Paradise. Even so, the observance of the Sabbath should be guarded by well-considered legislative enactments, but it must never be imagined that the primary obligation to avoid disturbing the public order necessary for the sanctification of the Sabbath originates in the legislature, or that by Act of Parliament it can be relaxed or straitened. That lies beyond the scope of human authority.

Let me also repeat that the Divine law is not satisfied by

a mere cessation from labour. To take the text of Genesis, of the Decalogue, or of the Book of Nehemiah, and to surround that text with explanatory glosses is as precarious a service as can be well imagined. Such glosses may appear to be exact and clear enough, but experience tells us that they may at the same time be trifling, and the presumption of the authors is probably punished by the contempt which the minuteness of their exposition of the Heavenly Statute is likely to provoke. This does not, as I venture to believe, so much arise from any great obliquity in the views of wise and holy commentators, as from the incompetence of us all to make the sacred text clearer than it is, if men would but read it with the simplicity of common sense, and with a sincere willingness to do as God commands.

While I have pursued the thread of my inquiry in the preceding pages, I have not felt my own incompetence so deeply as I feel it now that I am attempting to close the book with a few practical observations, which I trust will be perused with candid consideration, and pray that the Author of the law itself may graciously assist me to perceive the spirit of it.

We gather from the original account of the Sabbath, as it was appointed at the beginning of the world, that it was to be a cessation from *ordinary daily business*. They, therefore, who would sanctify the day and keep it holy must not only abstain from manual labour—from that one kind of work which is sometimes called servile—but from those occupations which, taken altogether, make up their *business*. Some men's business tends to elevate the mind and character, some to depress, and some even to deprave. Apart from the thought of Sabbath sanctification, and looking only at every-day business in the light of God's own perfect works, and in the prospect of eternity, it should be such as can be done with a good conscience. If the business of any man, or any woman, has been to minister to vice, to pander to the idleness or dishonesty of others, nothing that can be done on Sunday, under the name of religion, will procure a blessing on their craft. Tales are told of Romish devotions paid by thieves to the Virgin Mary, or to some other saint, in hope of compromising for the sin to be committed, or of the merit of a prayer or the consideration of an offering to avert the wrath of God; it is no less absurd or wicked for any one to suppose that by shutting up a fraudulent or a licentious business on Sunday he could purify it from its filthiness on working days. No day's devotions can sanctify the thing that is unholy. It must be supposed, while treating the present subject, that the reader's business or profession is as honest and pure a calling as can be. Yet it is only *his* business. It relates to this world, and may be innocently suspended, whenever necessary, or, always six days out of seven, innocently, honourably, and laudably pursued. He may earn a livelihood by it, or he may not. Perhaps he has retired from business, as we say, and therefore could suspend it altogether without any temporal inconvenience. He has, however, some pursuit; if it were only to drive away idleness, to preserve health, to comply with the ordinary usages of society, to fulfil the rites of hospitality, to render some service to his neighbour, to mingle usefully with his fellow-citizens—he must have some daily engagements. All this, then, is *what he has to do*, and he must do it in six days, and with that be satisfied. It is *his* work. The other day—Sunday, we will say, the Lord's-day—belongs to God, and on that day God's work is to be done, and God's only. This is what I have endeavoured to point out in the course of exposition, and on this I must now very earnestly insist.

Convenience will often be pleaded in excuse of doing things not strictly necessary; but while convenience may always be taken into account, convenience in matters of conscience must not be the first thing considered. Convenience is so entirely relative, that it must wait until duty and conscience are kept clear of prejudice by unseasonable concessions to what, for the occasion, may take its name. Perhaps this convenience turns out to be in reality an apology for business, or a concession to it, and in that case it must be put off until the days when business undisguised can be attended to.

Necessity has higher claims, but that for which necessity is pleaded is not always necessary. Certain petty indulgences, which have been long indulged in, are mistaken for necessities. So are compliances with fashion, custom, taste. The spendthrift indulges in extravagances until the day of his ruin. With some persons the alleged necessities are crimes. These are always, if we must speak so as to be understood, damnable, whatever be the day of the week. But on the Lord's-day, nothing is necessary that can not be done without a breach of what is plainly right according to a fair and honest reading of the Sabbath law.

Pleasure-taking cannot be called business, but it is utterly inconsistent with sanctification of the day, which is what God requires, what He rewards, and what is absolutely essential to our peace of mind, prosperity, and real happiness. Amusements, pleasure-parties, needless visits, worldly conversation, whatever withdraws the mind and steals the time from sanctification of the day, will be found contrary to the intent of many passages of Holy Scripture which, on the present subject, have all the force of law.

Against this it may be urged that many persons, not to say most persons, are so worldly as to be incapable of religious conversation, and insensible to the holy pleasure of devotion. This is true—too true. They live without God in the world, and if nothing can be expected from them but what is worldly, so much the worse, so much the greater is

L

their guilt. For such persons it is right to pray, and hope that they will not long continue to be what they are. Meanwhile God's law and their duty remain unchanged.

Parents and masters, tenderly concerned for those under their care, are often perplexed on these points. To them there is much to be said in regard to the entire circle of their duties, and there is much that they should have learned well before the season for perplexity arrived. They, if any, may be encouraged to allure their children and their servants into a regard for the service of God, until duty comes to be their delight. But, after all, his commandments are imperative, and even if it costs much trouble to bend our will into obedience, or to inculcate on those under our care the submission which it is their bounden duty to render to Almighty God, our own duty also must be discharged. Obedience is honourable in all, and must not be withheld. " To obey " is better than sacrifice, and to hearken than the fat of " rams." Unquestioning obedience must be given to God. The breath of our nostrils is not our own. Our life is in his hands. From him only will proceed the final sentence on which will irrevocably depend the settlement of the last awful question whether it shall be life or death eternal?— Heaven or Hell? The Sabbath-breaker, no less than other transgressors of his laws, must be reminded of this truth without hesitation or abatement.

If the Sabbath law were to be sought among the statutes of the realm, it would be entitled to respect. But it is written in the Bible, and therefore it is Divine, and of universal and absolute obligation. If it is not, then the first elements of morality are lost, and to keep or to break those primary laws which throw their sanctions around society, and make life itself sacred, is but optional, and all moral securities have ceased.

The exaggerated and unpractical view of Sabbath observance sometimes attributed to those who are called in derision Sabbatarians, is quite inconsistent with the convictions prevailing in circles where family religion best flourishes, and where Christian congregations abound in holy activity and influence.

A very scrupulous but sincere conscience, too scantily informed, guided by stern Puritanical examples, superstitiously avoiding the least bodily exertion that might look like work, abstaining from the most ordinary comforts, and punishing all around by enforcing ascetic abstinences and tedious devotions, is the ideal of a wearisome Sabbath devotee which some persons are pleased to hold up to derision. The prototype of such a character cannot be found in Scripture, and it is so absurd that there cannot be many examples of it in reality.

The fact is that the most faithful observers of the law of Scripture are among the happiest of mankind. They do indeed abstain from servile work, and they and their families rest entirely from worldly labour. But they do God's work, and therein they often labour hard, and yet awake cheerful and refreshed every Monday morning to resume their ordinary duties for the week. They know that there are works of piety which require very great exertion, and must be performed at any cost even on the Sabbath-day. They rightly conclude from their knowledge of the inspired Scriptures, and from the example of Christ, that no effort should be spared to save life, to alleviate pain, to rescue from peril, to defend one's self from the assaults of violence, or his country from the aggression of an enemy. They know that the performance of these duties may involve sleepless care and exhausting labour, and believe that it should not be intermitted even on the Lord's-day. Multitudes of devoted Christians are every Sunday zealously engaged in ministering succour to the helpless, healing to the sick, and comfort to the mourner. Not less promptly on this holy day than on any other, they would hasten to rescue their fellow-men from the conflagration or the wreck, cost them what it might to do so, without the least fear of Sabbath-breaking, but rather choosing this holy, consecrated day for imitating their blessed Saviour in deeds of self-denying mercy. They do not wantonly or ostentatiously prefer the day for toilsome benevolence, if they have the power to choose, but, whenever necessary, they reverently follow the footsteps of our Heavenly Master.

Whether it is lawful to do good on the Sabbath-day or to do evil, to destroy life or to save it, cannot be a doubtful question to any well-instructed person who knows how Christ has answered it. But to needlessly defer the performance of even these duties until the day of rest, and then to sally forth in distracting haste to do what might have been done before, is plainly a transgression of a plain law for the sake of what may thus become no better than a doubtful duty.

Doubts do indeed arise, and will not be disregarded by conscientious persons, but rather met and discussed with care, until they can be fairly solved—yet not in too great haste. They must be treated with delicacy, of course, yet handled with the utmost firmness, and solved with the greatest care, for whatsoever is not of faith is sin, if submitted to while it yet is doubtful.

There can be no doubt as to the end for which this weekly remission from toil is afforded. It is not for the sake of recreation only, for that would imply idleness, with all its consequences. On the contrary, a day which has been set apart from the Creation, by the command of God, should be distinguished from other days in a manner worthy of him to whom it is consecrated, and to whom, therefore, it belongs. It is a day for thankful commemoration and for reverential service. It is not enough that the service of such a day should be negative—a mere abstinence from business and pleasure; it must be an active service, a cheerful and holy consecration. The due commemoration of his works who is Creator of the universe, and Father and Redeemer of all mankind, when made by men who are conscious of their relation to him, and their redemption by him from the curse and penalty of sin, cannot be merely formal. The acts of true worship, which consist of fervent praises, confessions, and supplications, cannot be heartless. The satisfaction enjoyed by sincere worshippers cannot be less than heavenly. An unreal Sabbath, after all that we have read in the Bible, would be no better than a stupid mockery; an unfeeling and reluctant submission to its restraints would be senseless irreligion.

We know that to *remember* the day and also to *keep it holy* are the terms of an express command. We know that on this day we are entrusted with the golden opportunity for renewing our spiritual strength, resting from the drudgery of this world's care, and gaining fresh power for the discharge of every duty. We also know that for the observance or the breach of the command we must answer at the last great day of judgment. Each one of us in his own position as a parent, a master, a minister of Christ, or in whatever other relation to his Church, his country, or the world, is responsible for the example he is giving. He may not have any power to control others, nor any right to dictate precisely what each of them should do or should refrain from doing; but his example and his influence have weight, whether for good or evil, and, whether he knows it or not, he is building up or he destroys.

A writer on this vitally important subject should not fail to remind his readers that the law of God is not to be trifled with, but must, once and ever, be taken as the rule of life.

The Sabbath is now, no less than in the times of the prophets, the sign of a covenant between God and his people, whereby they are known who fear and love him, and honourably distinguished from those who live in open contempt of his authority.

To maintain this distinction clearly, without falling into the casuistic trifling which characterized the Pharisees—without peddling with mint and anise and cummin, while neglecting the weightier matters of the law—is just the point of practical Christian perfection to be aimed at. The task is just difficult enough to keep conscience awake and to test principle. There is a little difficulty, and the presence of such a difficulty may perhaps be compared with the sight of one forbidden tree in Paradise, the one tree of which the tillers and keepers of the garden might not eat. But the maintaining a normal principle is easy enough to any willing mind. There is a margin of discretion between things manifestly forbidden, and things freely allowed. There is such a margin, certainly, but it must not be trodden out into too great a width, and within its limit there will be no transgression of that principle.

For example: Buying and selling is comprehended under the general designation of *Business*, and all business is to be suspended on the Sabbath-day. But if a way-worn, hungry stranger craves for food of him who sells, the question may fairly rise in the conscience of the seller whether in such a case he ought not to exercise hospitality, and the stranger, having conscience also, may consider how he can fitly recompense. The sick may press for healing, and the seller of medicine must not withhold, and, as diseases do not wait, the druggist and the physician may not refuse to minister the means of healing. On this matter the teaching of Holy Scripture is clear enough. But if the idle clamour for entertainment, the drunkards for drink, the licentious for pandering to their appetites, all this lies so deeply within the region of evil, that it should be no man's trade at any time to help them. On Sunday, it is unquestionable that all ordinary business, having occupied six days of the seven, should in mercy be suspended; but to suspend that, and at the same time to throw open the gates of hurtful traffic, is not mere insanity, it is worse. It is open sin. It is a curse and scandal in a Christian country. Still, within the margin of things questionable, we find fair scope for Christian discretion. For the guidance of the family, or for the good order of the public, it is generally easy to arrive at a right conclusion; and if we do but consult God's Holy Word, and have recourse to intelligent reflection and to prayer, we shall not wander far out of the right way. "Consider what "I say," wrote St. Paul to Timothy, "and the Lord give "thee understanding in all things."

It is very pleasant to testify how much true Christians enjoy the sacred rest and solemn worship of the Lord's-day, and it is congenial with our best feelings to invite others to share with them in these enjoyments. Millions of witnesses rejoice to attest the blessedness of habitual Sabbath-keeping, and to declare how much its holy occupations contribute to prepare them for the eternal Sabbatism which remains for the people of God. But the present writer finds himself compelled to forego the pleasure of dwelling on this aspect of the subject. He hears it contended by many that the Sabbath is set aside by Christianity; that, although it is a beneficial institution to those who can make use of it, the observance of one day more than another is no longer obligatory, and that it is part of Christian liberty to do without it. He has, therefore, endeavoured to demonstrate by purely historical evidence that the law which they suppose to have been superseded by the Gospel is of sovereign, universal, and perpetual obligation. He believes that in the present state of opinion every one who fears God and believes the Bible to contain the revelation of God's truth and will, should take a firm stand on the only sure ground that is, and, abiding by the declared authority of our Lord Jesus Christ and his inspired servants, should maintain that the Gospel of Salvation does not abrogate the moral law of God. He must insist that Christians are not exempted from obedience to the very first commandment that issued from the Creator of the world, and is demonstrated to be of universal obligation. He believes it to be established beyond successful contradiction that it is necessary to the welfare of men in every land, and will continue to be necessary to the latest age.

The experience of mankind confirms our assurance that in keeping this commandment there is great reward, and it must ever be most emphatically said that it is *holy, just, and good.*

NEW WORKS AND NEW EDITIONS

PUBLISHED BY

S. W. PARTRIDGE & CO.,

9, PATERNOSTER ROW, LONDON.

The SALOON SHOW ROOM is open daily from Ten till Six. Saturday till Two.

INTRODUCTION TO THE STUDY OF THE BIBLE. By Rev. Joseph Baylee, D.D., late Principal of St. Aidan's College, Birkenhead. Second Edition. 3 vols. Demy 8vo, cloth, 21s.

VERBAL INSPIRATION the True Characteristic of God's Holy Word. By the same Author. Crown 8vo, cloth, 1s. 6d.

THE PEERAGE OF POVERTY; or, Learners and Workers in Fields, Farms, and Factories. By E. Paxton Hood, Author of "Self Formation," "Blind Amos," &c. Demy 8vo, cloth, 7s. 6d.

BYE-PATH MEADOW. By the same Author. Coloured Frontispiece, crown 8vo, cloth, 3s. 6d.

THE ROYAL MERCHANT; or, Events in the days of Sir Thomas Gresham, Knight, as narrated in the Diary of Ernst Verner, whilom his Page and Secretary, during the reigns of Mary and Elizabeth. By W. H. G. Kingston, Esq. Author of "The Martyr of Brentwood," &c. With Portrait, crown 8vo, cloth, 6s. 6d.

LECTURES ON ST. PAUL'S EPISTLE TO THE EPHESIANS. By the Rev. William Graham, D.D., Bonn, Prussia, Author of "On Spiritualising Scripture," "The Spirit of Love," &c. Crown 8vo, cloth, 7s. 6d.

REFLECTIONS ON CANTICLES; or, The Song of Solomon. With Illustrations from Modern Travellers and Naturalists. Crown 8vo, cloth. 3s. 6d.

THE JEWS; their Past, Present, and Future: being a succinct History of God's Ancient People in all Ages; with the Origin of the Talmud, and the Numbers of Jews in all Countries of the World. By J. Alexander. Small 8vo, 2s. 6d.

THE TRUE RIGHTS OF WOMAN. By Fanny Aiken Kortright. Second Edition. Demy 8vo, 1s. 6d.

DAY-BREAK IN ITALY. A Tale of the Italian Reformation. By E. Leslie. Coloured Frontispiece, crown 8vo, cloth, 3s. 6d.

ANCIENT MEETING-HOUSES; or, Memorial Pictures of Nonconformity in Old London. By G. H. Pike. Crown 8vo, cloth, 7s. 6d.

NOTES OF SERMONS by the late Rev. John Offord, Minister of Palace Gardens Chapel, Kensington. Crown 8vo, cloth, 3s. 6d.

LIGHTHOUSES AND BEACONS on the Voyage of Human Life. By Rev. J. Dickerson Davies, M.A. Fcap. 8vo, cloth, 3s.

TRUTH AND ERROR; A Calm Examination of the Doctrines of the Church of Rome. Fcap. 8vo, cloth, 2s.; gilt, 3s.

ON SPIRITUALISING SCRIPTURE; the Confessions of a Millenarian. By Rev. William Graham, D.D., Bonn, Prussia, Author of "The Spirit of Love," &c. Fcap., cloth, 1s. 6d.

THE SYRIAN LEPER; or, Sin and its Cure. By the Rev. Charles Bullock, Rector of St. Nicholas, Worcester; Editor of "Our Own Fireside," &c. With Frontispice. Fcap. 8vo, cloth, 2s. 6d.

THE MOTHER'S FAMILY PRAYER BOOK; or, A Help to Family Worship. Designed for use in the absence of Fathers and Heads of Households. By the Author of "Light Beyond." Crown 8vo, cloth, 3s. 6d.

SUNDAY READINGS FOR A YEAR; or, Two Hundred and Fifty Scripture Titles and Symbols of Christ. By James Large. Crown 8vo, cl., 5s.

THE MINISTRY OF WOMAN, and the London Poor. By A. V. L. Introduction by Mrs. Bayly, Author of "Ragged Homes," &c. Crown 8vo, cloth, gilt edges, 3s. 6d.

THE CORN OF WHEAT DYING AND BRINGING FORTH MUCH FRUIT. A Sketch of the Life of Capt. Allen Gardiner, R.N. By the Rev. Chas. Bullock, Editor of "Our Own Fireside." Crown 8vo, cloth, 1s. 6d.

A REPLY TO COBBETT'S "HISTORY OF THE REFORMATION IN ENGLAND AND IRELAND." Compiled and Edited by Charles Hastings Collette. Demy 8vo, cloth, pp. 350. 5s.

"ONE HUNDRED GRIEVANCES." A Chapter from the History of Pre-Reformation Days. By the same Editor. Demy 8vo, 2s.

A SAVIOUR FOR CHILDREN, and other Sermons for Little Folk. By James Dunckley. Crown 8vo, cloth, 3s. 6d.

ENGLAND OR ROME. The Re-union of Christendom; or, Halting between Two Opinions. By a Layman of the Church of England. Cloth, 3s. 6d.

THE GOSPEL TREASURY, and Practical Exposition of the Harmony of the Four Evangelists. Compiled by R. Mimpriss. Library Edition. Large type, Demy 4to, 1100 pages. Fifth Thousand. Cloth, 16s.; half calf, 22s.; whole calf, 30s. (Also publishing in sixteen monthly shilling parts. Part VI. now ready.)—Crown 8vo. edition, 950 pages. 27th thousand. Cloth, 6s.; calf gilt, 8s. 6d.; morocco, 10s.

TIM DOOLAN, the Irish Emigrant: Being a full and particular Account of his Reasons for Emigrating—His Passage across the Atlantic—His Arrival in New York—His brief Sojourn in the United States, and his further Emigration to Canada. By the Author of "Mick Tracy." With Frontispiece. Second edition. Crown 8vo, cloth, 3s. 6d.

THE PILGRIM'S PROGRESS FROM THIS WORLD TO THAT WHICH IS TO COME. By John Bunyan. With Memoir by Rev. W. Landels, D.D. Fcap. 4to, printed in clear type, with 74 coloured engravings. Elegant cloth, 5s.

THE LIFE OF JESUS. For Young People. By the Editor of "Kind Words." Profusely Illustrated with Original Engravings by J. and G. Nicholls. Crown 8vo, cloth, gilt edges, 5s.

"THE WHOLE ARMOUR OF GOD." An Explanation of the Christian Conflict, and the Divine Panoply therefor. By Lieut.-Gen. Goodwyn, Author of "Antitypical Parallels," &c. Crown 8vo, cloth, 2s. 6d.

"GATHER UP THE FRAGMENTS." Notes of Bible Classes. By C. P. Vol. I., Cloth, 2s. 6d.; Vol. II., 1s. 6d.

A DEVOUT SOLDIER: a Memoir of James Field. With Portraits, Map, and Illustrations. Crown 8vo, cloth, gilt edges, 3s. 6d.

THE GREAT ANTICHRIST. WHO? WHEN? WHERE? A Contribution for Anxious Times. By Rev. W. J. Bolton, M.A., Author of Hulsean Prize Essay for 1852, &c. With Lithographic Frontispiece. Crown 8vo, cloth, 1s. 6d.

CHRIST IN THE PENTATEUCH; or, Things Old and New concerning Jesus. By H. Bourn, Author of "Black Diamonds," &c. Crown, 8vo, cloth, 5s.

GOD'S PURPOSE IN JUDGMENT: considered with Especial Reference to the Assertion of Mercy or Annihilation for the Lost. By Robert Baxter, Esq. 16mo, cloth, 1s. 6d.

CONVERSATIONS ON THE BOOK OF REVELATION. Being a simple Exposition for the Young, according to the Views of the Rev. John Cumming, D.D., and the Rev. E. B. Elliott. By M. L. Yorke Draper. Fcap. 8vo, cloth, 5s.

THE PASTOR'S WIFE: a Memoir of Mrs. Sherman, of Surrey Chapel. By her Husband. With Portrait. Thirteenth Thousand. Cloth, 3s. 6d.

THE TIME OF THE END: Its Antecedents and its Character. By the Rev. Joseph Baylee, D.D., Late Principal of St. Aidan's Theological College, Birkenhead. Author of "The Intermediate State of the Blessed Dead." 8vo, cloth, 8s. 6d.

THE ROAD TO ROME, via OXFORD; or, Ritualism identical with Romanism. By Rev. J. A. Wylie, LL.D., Author of "The Papacy," &c. Crown 8vo, cloth, 5s.

AN INTRODUCTION TO THE READING AND STUDY OF THE ENGLISH BIBLE. By W. Carpenter. 3 vols., cloth, 16s. (or in 12 parts, 1s. 6d. each).

ANCIENT LANDMARKS; or, The Chief Lessons of the Epistles to the Ephesians, Philippians, Colossians, and Thessalonians. By J. M. Denniston, M.A. Crown 8vo, cloth, 3s. 6d.

SELF-FORMATION; or, Aids and Helps to Mind-Life. By E. Paxton Hood, Author of "Peerage of Poverty," &c. New Edition. Fcap. 8vo, cloth, 3s. 6d.

BLIND AMOS AND HIS VELVET PRINCIPLES; or Proverbs and Parable for the Young Folk. By the same Author. New Edition. Crown 8vo, Coloured Frontispiece and Title, cloth, 1s. 6d.

S. W. PARTRIDGE AND CO.'S FIVE-SHILLING SAMPLE PACKET OF SMALL GOSPEL BOOKS, for wide distribution. Seventy-two various. Sent free on receipt of stamps.

ANTITYPICAL PARALLELS; or, The Kingdom of Israel and of Heaven. With Notes, Illustrations, and Maps of the Original Occupation of Palestine, and of the Millennial Kingdom. By Lieut.-General Goodwyn. Royal 8vo, cloth, 16s.

"THE LAST ADAM." By the same Author. Crown 8vo, cloth, 3s. 6d.

THE "GREATER THAN SOLOMON." Twelve Lectures on the First Four Chapters of the Sacred Book of Canticles. By Rev. S. Allen Windle. 1s. 6d. Cloth, 2s.; gilt edges, 2s. 6d.

HOME AND SCHOOL MELODIES. Part I.—Forty American Sabbath-School Songs. Part II.—Forty American Revival and Home Songs. Part III.—Forty American Sabbath-School Songs. Part IV.—Forty Sacred Songs for Sabbath Schools, by W. Montgomery. Oblong 4to, 1s. each.

THE TEMPERANCE BIBLE COMMENTARY: giving at One View, Version, Criticism, and Exposition, in regard to all Passages of Holy Writ in which "Wine" or "Strong Drink," or illustrative of the Principles of the Temperance Reformation, are mentioned. By Dr. Lees and Dawson Burns. Second Edition. Demy 8vo, cloth, 6s.

ISRAEL'S EVENTIDE, and the Bright Dawn of the Eternal Day. By Rev. J. G. Gregory, M.A., Minister of Park Chapel, Chelsea, late Rector of Bonchurch. Fourth Edition. Fcap 8vo, cloth, 4s. 6d.

THE BELIEVER SUFFERING; or, Comfort, Warning, and Counsel to those in Trouble. Fcap. 8vo, cloth, 2s. 6d.

THE REVELATION UNRAVELLED. An Outline Exposition on a New Plan. By Author of the "Coming Crisis." With Preface by Rev. R. Chester. 12mo, cloth, 2s. 6d.

THE FUTURE OF EUROPE. What will it be? and will France be the Leading Power? A Historic and Prophetic Search. By T. Ryan. Third Edition. Crown 8vo. 1s.

HYMNS OF LIFE AND PEACE. By J. Denham Smith. Impl. 16mo, cloth, 2s. 6d.

MUSIC FOR TIMES OF REFRESHING HYMN-BOOK. With Appendix. Edited by J. Denham Smith. Small 4to, red edges, 3s. 6d.

WINNOWED GRAIN; or, Selections from the Addresses of the Rev. J. Denham Smith. *Cheaper edition.* Demy 16mo. Third edition. Cloth, 1s. 6d.

LONDON AND BRIGHTON ADDRESSES. By Rev. J. Denham Smith. 16mo, cloth, gilt, 1s. (Or in Four Penny Nos.)

LIFE AND WALK: Seven Addresses. By the same Author. Demy 16mo, cloth, 1s. 6d.

LIFE TRUTHS. By the same Author. 16mo, cloth, 1s. 6d.; gilt, 2s. (People's Edition, 6d.)

LIFE IN CHRIST. By the same Author. 16mo, cloth, 1s. 6d.; gilt 2s.

HYMN-WRITERS AND THEIR HYMNS. By Rev. S. W. Christophers. Post 8vo, cloth, red edges, 7s. 6d.

RECONCILIATION; or, How to be Saved. By Rev. W. Taylor, of California. Crown 8vo, cloth, 1s.; 2s. 6d.; gilt, 3s. 6d.

THE INFANCY AND MANHOOD OF CHRISTIAN LIFE. By the same Author. Crown 8vo, cloth, 1s., 2s. 6d.; gilt, 3s. 6d.

HENRY VIII.: an Historical Sketch, as affecting the Reformation in England. By C. H. Collette. Royal 8vo, paper, 1s.

"THE CRUSHER" AND THE CROSS. A Narrative of a Remarkable Conversion. By A. Fergusson, Author of "Life's By-ways," &c. Crown 8vo, cloth, 2s. 6d.

PRECIOUS TRUTHS FOR EVERY ONE. Imperial 32mo. 16th thousand, limp cloth, 1s.; cloth, red edges, 1s. 6d.

EVERY-DAY WONDERS OF BODILY LIFE; essential to be known for Health and Comfort. By Anne Bullar. Eighth Thousand. Fcap. 8vo, cloth, 1s.

LOST AND FOUND; a Temperance Tale. By the Author of "Jane Grey's Resolution," &c. Royal 16mo, 2s.

THE HYMNS OF HEAVEN; or, The Songs of the Saints in Glory. By James Grant, Author of "Our Heavenly Home," &c. Foolscap, cloth, 2s. 6d.

THE PRECIOUSNESS OF CHRIST; or, Meditations on the Person and Work of the Lord Jesus. By Rev. H. Knapp, Curate of St. Helen's and Sea View, Isle of Wight. 18mo, cloth, 1s. 6d.

ST. MARY'S CONVENT; or, Chapters in the Life of a Nun. By the Author of "Thady D'Arcy," &c. Foolscap 8vo, cloth, 2s. 6d.

THE TEST OF TRUTH: an Argument and a Narrative. By Mary Jane Graham. Ninth Edition. Royal 32mo, cloth gilt, 1s. (or separate, 6d. each.)

"MARY DON'T HEAR US!" With four Illustrations. Square 16mo, cloth, 1s.

ENGLISH DERIVED FROM HEBREW; with Glances at Greek and Latin. By R. Govett. Demy 8vo, cloth, 4s.

A CONCORDANCE OF THE HOLY SCRIPTURES, with One or more References to every Verse, except the Lists of Names. Compiled by Rev. Thomas Snow, Halifax. Royal 16mo, limp cloth, 1s. 6d.; cloth, red edges, 2s.

THE PASTOR AND THE PARISH; or, The Minister as Preacher, Pastor, Catechist, &c. By John B. Heard, M.A., Perpetual Curate of Bilton, Harrogate. (One Hundred Guinea Essay.) Crown 8vo, cloth, 3s. 6d.

THE DOWN-HILL OF LIFE; its Exercises, Temptations, and Dangers. With the effectual Method of Rendering the Descent Safe and Easy, and its Termination Triumphant. By Rev. T. H. Walker, Author of " Good Wives, Good Servants, and Happy Homes," &c. Crown 8vo, cloth, 1s. 6d.

SCRIPTURE TEACHINGS FOR YOUNG CHILDREN. By Elizabeth C. Ashby. Old Testament. Royal 16mo, cloth, 1s. 6d.

SCRIPTURE TEACHINGS FROM THE NEW TESTAMENT. By the same Author. Royal 16mo, cloth, 1s. 6d.

THE EVANGELICAL HYMN-BOOK. 32mo, 1s. 6d., 2s., 3s.; 18mo, 3s., 4s. 6d.

THE JAPANESE EMPIRE; its Physical, Political, and Social Condition and History. By S. B. KEMISH. Crown 8vo, cloth, 3s. 6d.

GOSPEL ECHOES; or, Help to the Heralds of Salvation. By A. Midlane. 3d.; 6d.; 1s.

HEART MELODIES, AND LIFE LIGHTS. By A. M. H., Authoress of " The Life Look," &c. Square 18mo, cloth, 1s.

COUNSELS AND KNOWLEDGE FROM THE WORDS OF TRUTH. By Rev. F. Whitfield, M.A. Crown 8vo, cloth, 3s. 6d.

SPIRITUAL UNFOLDINGS FROM THE WORD OF LIFE. By the same Author. Second Edition. Crown 8vo, cloth, 3s. 6d.

THE WORD UNVEILED. By the same Author. Crown 8vo, cloth, 3s. 6d.

TRUTH IN CHRIST. By the same Author. Second Edition. Crown 8vo, cloth, 3s. 6d.

GLEANINGS FROM SCRIPTURE. By the same Author. Third Edition. Crown 8vo, cloth, 3s. 6d.

VOICES FROM THE VALLEY TESTIFYING OF JESUS. By the same Author. Fifth Edition. Crown 8vo, cloth, 3s. 6d.

THE HARMONY OF SCIENCE AND FAITH; an Attempt to Ascertain how far Belief in the Bible is affected by Modern Scientific Discovery. By the Author of " The Bible in the Workshop." Crown 8vo, cloth, 6s.

HEAVENWARD HO! or, Homeward Bound. A Seaman's Sunday Book. Second Edition. Crown 8vo, limp cloth, 1s.

CHARLES WESLEY, THE POET OF METHODISM. With List of his Poetical Works, and Autographs of Two Original Hymns. Cloth 1s.

SELECTED SERMONS. By the late Rev. James Bolton, B.A., Minister of St. Paul's Episcopal Chapel, Kilburn. Second Series. With Photograph Portrait. Crown 8vo cloth 5s.

MICK TRACY, the Irish Scripture Reader. With Engravings. Twelfth Thousand. Crown 8vo, cloth, 3s. 6d.

THE MODEL PARISH. A Prize Essay on the Pastoral Character and Pastoral Work. By F. R. Wynne, A. B., Incumbent of St. Mary's, Kilkenny. (Fifty Guinea Essay.) Crown 8vo, cloth, 3s. 6d.

MORNING DEWDROPS; or, The Juvenile Abstainer. By Mrs. Balfour. Fifth Edition, enlarged. Crown 8vo, cloth, 3s. 6d.

GEMS FOR THE AFFLICTED. Third Edition. Royal 32mo, 6d.; cloth, gilt, 1s.

WON AT LAST; and Bianchi, the Pedlar. 18mo, 6d.; gilt, 1s.

THE ROYAL RIGHTS OF THE LORD JESUS. By Rev. Dr. Leask. Crown 8vo, cloth, 3s. 6d.

HAPPY YEARS AT HAND; Outline of the Coming Theocracy. By the same Author. Second Thousand. Crown 8vo, cloth, 4s.

"A GOOD MAN, A VERY GOOD MAN INDEED," &c. By Rev. J. de Liefde, Amsterdam. 18mo, 6d. Cloth, 1s.

THE DUBLIN TRACTS. Pursuant to a recent reduction, a large Sample packet of these tracts may (for gratuitous distribution) be had for 10s. Complete lists on application.

THE STIRLING TRACTS. The entire Series of these Tracts is now kept in Stock, and complete lists may be had on application.

BRITISH MESSENGER, Part for 1862. Paper, 1s. 6d.; cloth, 2s. Part for 1863, 1s. 6d. Cloth, 2s. Parts for 1864 to 1869, paper, 1s. 6d. each.

THE PICTORIAL MISSIONARY NEWS. Four Annual Volumes. Pictorial Covers, 2s. 6d. each; cloth, gilt edges, 4s. each; or the same in 2 Vols., handsome binding, 8s. 6d. each.

EIGHT LECTURES ON PROPHECY. From Shorthand Notes, with Corrections and Additions by the Authors. Fifth Edition, revised, 12mo, 1s.; gilt, 1s. 6d.

OUR ENGLISH MONTHS; a Poem on the Seasons in England. By S. W. Partridge. Crown 8vo, cloth, 6s.; gilt, 7s. 6d; morocco, 10s. 6d.

UPWARD AND ONWARD; a Thought Book for the Threshold of Active Life. By same Author. 7th Thousand. Cr. 8vo, cl., 4s.; gilt, 5s.; morocco, 8s.

LEVER LINES FOR SPARE MINUTES. By the same Author. Crown 8vo, limp cloth, 1s.

AN IDEA OF A CHRISTIAN. By the same Author. Third Thousand. Demy 8vo, cloth. 1s.

VOICES FROM THE GARDEN; or the Christian Language of Flowers. By the same Author. Fourth Thousand. Paper, gilt, 1s.; cloth gilt, 2s.

THE COMING GLORY; a Series of Brief Treatises on the Coming and Kingdom of Christ, revealed in the Sure Word of Prophecy. Cl. 6d.; gilt, 1s.

THE STEPS OF JESUS. A Narrative Harmony of the Four Evangelists, in the Words of the Authorised Version. With Map. By R. Mimpriss. New Edition. 18mo, cloth, 1s. 6d., 48mo, cloth, 8d.

MY SERMON REMEMBRANCER. (A blank book of upwards of 100 pp. for recording the heads of sermons, &c.) Royal 8vo, limp cloth, 1s.

OUR MAID SERVANTS. A few Friendly Hints and Counsels. By A. F. G. Crown 8vo, cloth, 1s.

GOLDEN TREASURES, gleaned from Writings of various Ages, illustrating the Gospel of God's Grace. Series I. to IV. 6d. each; cloth, 1s.

THE CHURCH OF ENGLAND TEMPERANCE MAGAZINE, 1864 to 1868, 4s. each; 1869, 1s. 6d.

BIBLICAL NOTES AND QUERIES. Half-yearly Vol. 2s.

FRIEND-IN-NEED PAPERS. Vol. for 1869. 1s. 6d. and 2s. 6d.

BOOKS FOR THE TIMES.

Crown 8vo, illustrated boards, 1s. each.

THE LAST LOOK. A Tale of the Spanish Inquisition. By W. H. Kingston, Esq.
COUNT ULRICH OF LINDBURGH; a Tale of the Reformation in Germany. By the same.
THE MARTYR OF BRENTWOOD; or 300 Years Ago. By the same.
MARGARET'S VENTURE. By the Author of "Jenny's Geranium."
THE O'TOOLES OF GLEN IMAAL. By Rev. G. R. Wynne.
THE CURATE OF WEST NORTON. By the same.
THE CONVERTS OF KILBANN. An Irish Story. By the same.
HENRY HILLIARD; or, The Three College Friends.
OVERTON'S QUESTION, AND WHAT CAME OF IT.
CAREY GLYNN; or, The Child Teacher. By Rev. Dr. Leask.

ROLLS FOR SICK ROOMS, ETC., IN LARGE TYPE.

The Family Instructor. Thirty-one Leaves of Selected Texts. 1s. 6d.
The Silent Comforter. Thirty Leaves of Selected Texts. 2s.
The Silent Comforter. Part II. Hymns. Thirty-one Leaves of Hymns. 2s.
Green Pastures. Thirty-one Leaves of Selected Texts. 6th Thousand. 2s.
Green Pastures. Part II. Hymns. Thirty Leaves of Selected Hymns. 2s.
Sayings of Jesus. Parts I. and II. 1s. each.
Words of Comfort. Twelve Leaves of Selected Texts. 6d.
Words of Life. Twelve Leaves of Selected Texts. 6d.

ILLUSTRATED BOOKS.

OUR DUMB NEIGHBOURS; or, Conversations of a Father with his Children on Domestic and other Animals. By Rev. T. Jackson, M.A. With numerous engravings. Cloth, 5s.; gilt, 7s. 6d.

JACK THE CONQUEROR; or Difficulties Overcome. By the Author of "Dick and his Donkey." With 12 full-page Engravings, cloth, 5s.; gilt, 7s. 6d.

CLEVER DOGS AND HORSES, with Anecdotes of other Animals. By Shirley Hibberd, Esq. With 24 full-page Engravings. Cloth, 5s.; gilt, 7s. 6d.

ANIMAL SAGACITY. A Selection of Remarkable Incidents illustrative of the Sagacity of Animals. In Prose and Verse. Edited by Mrs. C. Hall. With 75 Engravings. Cloth, 5s.; gilt, 7s. 6d.

OUR FOUR-FOOTED FRIENDS; or the History of Manor Farm. By Mary Howitt. With Fifty Engravings. Cloth, 5s.; gilt, 7s. 6d.

OUR DUMB COMPANIONS; or Conversations of a Father and his Children about Dogs, Horses, Cats, and Donkeys. By the Rev. Thomas Jackson, M.A. with Illustrations by Landseer, Ansdell, Herring, and Weir. Cloth, 5s.; gilt, 7s. 6d.

OUR CHILDREN'S PETS. By Josephine. With Illustrations by Harrison Weir, Birket Foster, &c. Small 4to; cloth, 5s.; gilt, 7s. 6d.

ILLUSTRATED SONGS AND HYMNS FOR THE LITTLE ONES. 160 Wood-cuts, from drawings after Sir E. Landseer, Gilbert, Birket Foster, Anelay, Harrison Weir, and Huard. One vol., cloth, 5s.; gilt, 7s. 6d.

MY MOTHER. By Ann Taylor. A Series of Twelve Oil Pictures. illustrative of this popular Nursery Poem. Cloth gilt, 5s.

BIBLE WONDERS. By Rev. Richard Newton, D.D. With many Illustrations. Cloth 1s. 6d.

TEXTS AND FLOWERS, Illuminated. A Series of Pen and Pencil Illustrations of Popular Flowers. Cloth gilt, 5s.; or in assorted Packets, 2s. 6d.

THE CHRISTIAN MONITOR; or Selections from Pious Authors. With numerous Illustrations. Crown 8vo, cloth, 2s. 6d.; gilt, 3s. 6d.

THE BRITISH WORKMAN. 15 Yearly parts (1855 to 1869). Coloured Cover, 1s. 6d. each; gilt edges, 2s. 6d. each. Five Years' Vols., 1855 to 1859, 9s. each, cloth. 1860 to 1864, and 1865 to 1869, 10s. 6d. each, gilt edges.

THE BAND OF HOPE REVIEW. 19 Yearly Parts (1851 to 1869). Stiff Cover, 1s. each. Ten Years' Vol., 1851 to 1860, cloth, 10s.; gilt edges, 12s. Five Years' Vol., 1861 to 1865, cloth, 5s.; gilt edges, 6s.

THE CHILDREN'S FRIEND. 9 Vols. (1861 to 1869). Coloured Covers, 1s. 6d.; cloth, 2s.; gilt edges, 2s. 6d. each; the Nine Years, 1861 to 1869, 8 Vols, cloth, 5s.; gilt edges, 6s. each.

INFANT'S MAGAZINE. 4 Vols. (1866 to 1869). Coloured Covers, 1s. 6d.; cloth, 2s.; gilt edges, 2s. 6d. each.

FRIENDLY VISITOR. Vols. 1867, 1868, 1869. Coloured Cover, 1s. 6d.; cloth, 2s.; gilt edges, 2s. 6d. each.

SERVANTS' MAGAZINE. 3 Vols. (1867 to 1869). Cloth, 1s. 6d.; gilt edges, 2s. each.

(Full Catalogues post-free for one stamp.)

LONDON : S. W. PARTRIDGE & CO., 9, PATERNOSTER ROW.

www.ingramcontent.com/pod-product-compliance
Lightning Source LLC
Chambersburg PA
CBHW030247170426
43202CB00009B/661